PRAISE FOR RWANDA, INC.

"In *Rwanda, Inc.*, Crisafulli and Redmond recount the rise of an unyielding people and their chief executive, President Paul Kagame. The Rwandans, rallying around their national pride, have built predictable systems that reward enterprise and hard work, and created an exceptional blueprint for other developing countries."

—President Bill Clinton

"Crisafulli and Redmond investigate the Rwandan renaissance, focusing on 'Rwanda's CEO,' Paul Kagame . . . a fascinating portrait of a nation and a president at a pivotal moment in history."

—*Publishers Weekly*

"An instructive snapshot of Rwanda today."

—*Kirkus Reviews*

"Andrea Redmond and Patricia Crisafulli are known for their ability to connect with people, examine leadership skills, and teach us through their compelling observations and insights. As advocates for the future of Rwanda, they are now telling a story that we can all benefit from hearing."

—Jamie Dimon, chairman and chief executive officer, JPMorgan Chase

"*Rwanda, Inc.* documents this beautiful country's ongoing transformation through the lens of leadership, capturing the resilience of the human spirit and the potential for any country—or company—to chart an ambitious new course with ingenuity, collaboration, pragmatism, and passion."

—Howard Schultz, chairman, president, and chief executive officer, Starbucks

"Paul Kagame is one of my heroes and I believe [he] should be recognized as a 'Hero of the World.' He has led Rwanda out of the most hellish nightmare one can imagine, into the daylight of national reconciliation and the formation of a democracy. This is a story that can become a model for the entire African continent."

—James Sinegal, cofounder and director, Costco

"Rwanda has achieved a remarkable turnaround, from the poster child of despair to symbol of progress, in less than 20 years. The unique leadership attributes of Rwandan President Kagame and his drive for broad-based economic growth continue to move the country forward. Rwanda today is inclusive, focuses on reconciliation, empowers women, decentralizes government, and involves the community in rebuilding—for the benefit of all. This is why Marriott wants to do business in Rwanda. Here, Crisafulli and Redmond tell this turnaround story brilliantly."

—Arne M. Sorenson, president and chief executive officer, Marriott International, Inc.

"By adopting an approach of 'trade not aid,' our company has developed a sustainable multi-million-dollar business relationship with Rwanda since 2005. Our beautiful, handmade Path to Peace baskets, sold in Macy's stores and on macys.com, help hundreds of widows of the genocide support themselves and their families. In *Rwanda, Inc.*, Patricia Crisafulli and Andrea Redmond outline how President Kagame rebuilt the Rwandan nation in a manner that encouraged business collaboration and projects like Path to Peace at Macy's. In the process, what was a tragedy has become a story of inspiration and hope, with all of the women of Rwanda working side by side."

—Terry J. Lundgren, chairman, president, and chief executive officer, Macy's, Inc.

RWANDA, INC.

HOW A DEVASTATED NATION BECAME AN
ECONOMIC MODEL FOR THE DEVELOPING WORLD

PATRICIA CRISAFULLI
AND ANDREA REDMOND

palgrave
macmillan

RWANDA, INC.
Copyright © Patricia Crisafulli and Andrea Redmond, 2012.

First published in 2012 by PALGRAVE MACMILLAN® in the U.S.—a
division of St. Martin's Press LLC, 175 Fifth Avenue, New York, NY
10010.

Where this book is distributed in the UK, Europe, and the rest of
the world, this is by Palgrave Macmillan, a division of Macmillan
Publishers Limited, registered in England, company number 785998, of
Houndmills, Basingstoke, Hampshire RG21 6XS.

Palgrave Macmillan is the global academic imprint of the above
companies and has companies and representatives throughout the
world.

Palgrave® and Macmillan® are registered trademarks in the United
States, the United Kingdom, Europe, and other countries.

ISBN: 978-0-230-34022-0

Library of Congress Cataloging-in-Publication Data

Crisafulli, Patricia.
    Rwanda, Inc. : how a devastated nation became an economic model
for the developing world / Patricia Crisafulli and Andrea Redmond.
        p.   cm.
    Includes index.
    ISBN 978-0-230-34022-0
    1. Rwanda—Economic policy. 2. Economic development—Rwanda.
3. Investments, Foreign—Rwanda. 4. Political leadership—Rwanda. 5.
Kagame, Paul, 1957– I. Redmond, Andrea. II. Title.
HC875.C75   2012
338.967571—dc23

                                                             2012017937

A catalogue record of the book is available from the British Library.

Design by Letra Libre, Inc.

First edition: November 2012

10   9   8   7   6   5   4   3   2   1

Printed in the United States of America.

*To the people of Rwanda, who continue to
demonstrate what is possible when vision
is combined with courage and commitment
and backed by exemplary leadership.*

CONTENTS

8 pages of photographs appear between pages 130 and 131.

FOREWORD

Joseph W. Saunders
Chairman and CEO, Visa Inc.

n December 2011 Visa Inc. and the government of Rwanda announced a groundbreaking agreement for both the company and the country of Rwanda: a partnership to electronify Rwanda's economy, which will help to connect the nearly 11 million residents of this country to the formal financial sector. The announcement was the end result of a long process for Visa, of studying innovative products that could be launched in emerging markets and choosing the country in which these new products would first be unveiled and tested.

While no country was perfect on all of Visa's measures, Rwanda distinguished itself quickly and clearly because of its pro-business attitude, zero tolerance for corruption, and a government that was very eager to partner with us in order to reach the 86 percent of the Rwandan population that lacks traditional financial services. For us, government support was paramount.

Our experience supports the premise of *Rwanda, Inc.*: that this country is in the midst of an amazing turnaround. In less than two decades it has gone from complete devastation after the genocide 18 years ago to impressive economic development, which has resulted in strong GDP growth that has lifted one million people out of poverty in the past five years alone. As the authors state, Rwanda is "the ultimate turnaround," which has been accomplished by having a clear vision and the commitment to execute a strategy that would make it a reality. For Visa, it is exciting to be part of the Rwandan business community and economic fabric.

Our partnership with Rwanda covers a full spectrum of services that are important to the country's economic growth strategy, including modernizing the payments network in the country, upgrading automated teller machines, installing more merchant card readers, and developing e-commerce. Visa's solutions will help tourists and business travelers in Rwanda to use credit or debit cards to pay for goods and services.

The Visa initiative also targets a new and very important customer base, which is also a priority for the Rwandan government: the millions of people who do not currently have access to reliable and convenient financial services. Enabling these individuals to better manage their financial lives through the combination of accessible branchless banking networks and ubiquitous mobile devices is a significant step toward bringing the benefits of Rwanda's economic expansion to even more of its citizens. Already, the country has over four million mobile phone users, a figure that is expected to grow to six million in the near term. Visa is capitalizing on this trend to provide simple alternatives to average Rwandans who, like all of us, crave convenient ways to save for education, pay monthly bills, and quickly send funds to friends and family.

However, an initiative of this scope can only be done with appropriate support, particularly with regard to education, which is a real passion for Visa and for me. Visa, in partnership with the government of Rwanda, has rolled out financial literacy programs that are tailored to a variety of audiences, from residents of rural communities to government workers and bank employees. Our intention is to make learning fun and engaging with messages interspersed in street theatre performances, popular music tapes played in commuter buses, and "Financial Football," a soccer-themed game based on financial education.

The Visa financial literacy initiative recognizes the thirst for knowledge and development within Rwanda, which intends to diversify its economy with emphasis on information and communication technology (ICT). The country has already made significant strides toward that goal by laying a fiber optic broadband network across the country: modern infrastructure to deliver the very best in education, healthcare, commerce—and financial services, too. These investments, combined with a commitment to delivering universal primary education (in English) and high quality post-secondary education options, are a testament to Rwanda's determination to become a middle income, knowledge-based economy. For Visa, the Rwandan partnership is a new way of doing business in emerging markets, but it is also, importantly, a commercial venture that will benefit Visa in terms of volume and revenue. That is essential for any private enterprise. It is an added bonus and a great satisfaction that Visa's work in Rwanda not only stands to do well, but can also do good, by expanding access to financial services and financial literacy to Rwandans. We are proud to partner with Rwanda as it strives to realize its dream of becoming an ICT-based knowledge economy.

When we looked to emerging economies around the world, Rwanda stood out as a clear choice for doing business. We hope that other companies will join us as they look for opportunities to reach new consumers in the vibrant and exciting African marketplace. Rwanda is open for business, and Visa is proud to be there.

ACKNOWLEDGMENTS

As we undertook the writing of this book, we were supported and assisted by so many people. The list is very long, indeed, and extends well beyond the names we can mention here. We would like to thank, in particular, the following individuals for their help and support.

For opening doors and making introductions: Dale Dawson, Tom Allen, Cheryl Mills, Debbie Harmon, Peter Scher, Judith Miller, Michael Fairbanks, Francis Gatare, Yolande Makolo, Keuria Sangwa, and Rose Kabuye.

For supporting this project in numerous ways: Toni Ficaro, who always goes above and beyond and was a true partner in this project; Penny Pritzker, for her support and friendship; and Ben Zastawny and Delia Berrigan Fakis, with our special thanks for their diligence and dedication. Also special thanks to Joe Saunders and Doug Michelman of Visa Inc.

For providing inspiration along the way: Jackie Karuletwa-Kaziza and Colin Muhoozi Kakiza; Bishop Laurent Mbanda and Bishop John Rucyahana; the artists at Uburanga and Ivuka galleries, including Richard Karekezi and Innocent Nkurunziza;

and the children at Sonrise School, including Jean-Claude and John of God.

For seeing the vision of this book from the beginning: our agent, Doris Michaels of DSM Agency; our editor, Emily Carleton, whose loving care is evident on each page; her assistant, Laura Lancaster, for helping to shepherd the process; Carla Benton, Lauren Dwyer, Andrew Varhol, and the entire Palgrave Macmillan team.

For our families and loved ones: Bill and Duke Ferguson, Ardis Redmond, Paul Redmond, (Andrea); and Joe Tulacz, Pat Commins, Bernadette and Stephanie Crisafulli, and Jeannie and Ben Zastawny, (Tricia). A special thanks to Bill Ferguson for support that cannot be measured in airline miles and travel expenses alone.

For the dedicated team at Bridge2Rwanda, in appreciation for all you do, including Dale Dawson, Tom Allen, Blayne Sharpe, Clay Parker, Anna Reed, and Richard Siegler.

For all those who agreed to be interviewed for this book, sharing their expertise as well as their personal stories; without you this book would not have been possible.

INTRODUCTION

This Is Rwanda

There is a joke among residents and frequent visitors to Kigali, the capital city of Rwanda, that if you blink twice, you will see a building that wasn't there just the other day. What seems like pure exaggeration became a reality for us over numerous trips made to this tiny, landlocked country in eastern Africa. Each time we arrived, there was something else to see. Tower cranes sprouted in new places along the skyline. A multistory hotel to be operated by a leading international hospitality brand went from a construction shell to near completion. Even traffic light installations began to tame Kigali's chaotic and sometimes heart-stopping traffic patterns.

As authors exploring the economic development of Rwanda and the leadership principles and governance structures that have brought it into being, we found evidence virtually everywhere. All around Rwanda, a new narrative is unfolding; one of self-determination and increasing self-reliance, and of a country in a hurry to get where it wants and needs to be. This new story is not meant to erase the 1994 genocide, which is what comes to mind when most people say the name *Rwanda*: a human-induced tragedy of catastrophic proportions, when a million or more people died in 100 days. But what is happening in Rwanda now will add another chapter to that story; out of the proverbial ashes, a nation of hope and possibility has arisen, taken root, and begun to flourish.

Our introduction to Rwanda came from an American non-governmental organization (NGO), Bridge2Rwanda, which focuses on education, servant leadership, and entrepreneurial ventures in the country. The founder, Dale Dawson, an American executive and former investment banker, was profiled in our previous book, *Comebacks*, which tells the stories of business leaders, mostly CEOs of large-cap companies, who suffered upsets in their careers, which we euphemistically referred to as "getting the rug pulled out." Dale, however, had pulled the rug out himself, leaving behind the success of his former career for the significance of making a difference in Rwanda. Through Bridge2Rwanda and its many connections, we came to know the country, its leaders, and those undertaking meaningful work in all sectors of society and the economy. But ours is an independent work, commissioned by no one and not officially sanctioned, although we had the cooperation of the Rwandan government and access to its leaders, including President Paul Kagame.

No one in the Rwandan government reviewed our drafts, nor did they even seek quote approval. (The only ones who asked for that courtesy were a few Westerners, mostly Americans.) Such access and transparency was not only gracious but courageous, particularly at a time when Rwanda has come under sharp criticism around issues of free speech and human rights. "Perception has a disproportionate effect on us," one member of the Kagame administration complained. Indeed, given all the ills of the modern world, tiny Rwanda draws outsized criticism. Yet this scrutiny is largely a by-product of its tremendous success, given its strong economic growth and track record of lifting people out of poverty. How Rwanda accomplished this tremendous achievement is the story we set out to tell.

Instead of remaining dependent on foreign aid postgenocide, Rwanda is determined to transform its economy from subsistence agriculture, which currently supports nearly 80 percent of the population, to a hub of information and communication technology (ICT). That goal alone would be audacious enough without everything else Rwanda must do at the same time: expanding compulsory education to twelve years, improving health care and reducing maternal and infant mortality, sustaining its newly achieved food security, promoting peace and stability in the midst of enemies who continue to threaten the country, and building and solidifying institutions that will stand up through the transition of government from its iconic leader to whoever comes next.

If these goals can be realized, then all that Rwanda has achieved thus far postgenocide will be overshadowed by the fulfillment of its future. As progress is made, slowly but steadily, credit is given to one man: President Paul Kagame. A study of his leadership in Rwanda reveals strong parallels to a corporate leader: his comprehensive vision, exacting attention to details, and drive for execution. Indeed, the way he leads Rwanda—as a pro–private sector, free market economy with governance structures that enhance transparency and uphold zero tolerance for corruption—draws comparison with a CEO. It also gave this book its title, *Rwanda, Inc.*

Not everyone, however, sees Rwanda as a success story. Once the darling of the Western press, which wrote glowing reports postgenocide, Rwanda has seen the pendulum of opinion in some circles swing in the other direction where the country and its leaders are concerned. Critics have emerged, vocal and opinionated. Some are former architects of the genocide and their supporters, who both want nothing more than to defeat Rwanda by undermining its current leadership and to reverse the progress made to unify people who embrace a national identity of being Rwandan. There are also the disaffected who have fallen out of favor and who now make it their purpose and their profession to criticize Rwanda at every turn. In addition, there are critics among watchdog groups because Rwanda fails to live up to their standards as discussion continues around free speech and human rights. Rwanda defends itself by citing the scars it still bears from the genocide and the simmering tensions that linger.

We acknowledge these voices, but our focus is not on them or their arguments. *Rwanda, Inc.* is not a political book, but one that focuses on economic development, governance, and leadership. Nor is *Rwanda, Inc.* meant to be a comprehensive history of the country or a biography of Paul Kagame.

Rwanda, Inc. begins with an overview we call "Rwanda Now: The Skyscraper and the Chicken," calling to mind two powerful symbols of Rwanda's ambitions for the future and its focus on the needs of all people, particularly those at the lowest socioeconomic level. Next we briefly explore Rwanda's past. To appreciate where Rwanda is today, one must understand where it has been, through civil war and genocide, during which a new leader emerged: Major General Paul Kagame, who led the Rwandan Patriotic Army, declined the presidency of the transitional government, and then accepted the position six years later. Today, he is completing his second democratically elected term, which he has pledged will be his last.

From devastation has come reconciliation and unification, twin goals that are absolutely crucial to Rwanda's pursuit of peace and prosperity. From there, we explore the leadership of "Rwanda's CEO," from Kagame's trademark discipline to his ability to see things not just as they are, but how they could be. We discuss the "Rwanda Model" for poverty reduction, a strategy of private sector–led development, decentralized government, transparency, and accountability at all levels. Implementing that model includes specific objectives, which we discuss in separate chapters: raising the bottom of the socioeconomic pyramid—through agriculture, education, and health care—and developing infrastructure, especially energy and large-scale transportation projects. In Rwanda on the world stage, we address the criticisms the country and its leadership faces and its arguments to counter them. In the last chapter, we discuss succession: the expectation that Kagame will step down in 2017 and the need to develop strong and highly capable leaders to bring Rwanda farther along its path toward greater development and progress.

To bring this story to life, we spoke with government officials, Rwandan business leaders, foreign investors, Westerners, NGOs, clergy, villagers, students, and anyone else who would talk to us. What emerged is a compelling portrait of a country charting its own course forward with determination and pride. Rwanda's vision for itself is infectious, and the possibility and even probability that it will meet its ambitious goals are very real. And yet there are drawbacks and challenges that cannot be overlooked, particularly where human capital is concerned. There are serious deficits in skills and experience that result in everything from bureaucratic delays in obtaining government approvals to disregard for sanctity of contract. Rwanda's learning curve is steep, but leadership is committed to closing the gaps.

In the midst of it all is President Kagame, who believes in results as the irrefutable truth that will emerge in time and show the world what Rwandans can accomplish economically, socially, and politically. A strong and determined leader, he has made an undeniable difference in his country.

There are two portraits of Kagame, as evident in the Western press. In one, he is a savior, nearly messianic in his mission and vision, who has single-handedly delivered the nation out of hell on earth. In the other, he is a heavy-handed tyrant, accused of acting like a dictator who silences the opposition. These two extremes became for us the left and right guardrails as we studied and analyzed his leadership. What we saw was a leader who was neither of the extremes; Kagame and the situations he faces are far too complex for that. He believes Rwanda's problems can only be solved with Rwandan solutions and, after seeing his country abandoned by the West during the genocide, cares little about international opinion. Yet, at the same time, he reaches out to partner with those who will help his country progress toward a better future for all Rwandans.

There are those who undoubtedly will say Rwanda's plans are commendable and its goals are inspiring, but then will add dismissively, "This is Africa," a jaded observation synonymous with "What else can you expect from this place?" The opinion still exists that nothing will ever change on a continent that has suffered from the ills of European colonialism, endemic corruption, and poor leadership. But what happens in one area of the continent is not fated by geography alone to occur on another. We would argue the change in Rwanda is both real and sustainable. This country, which is so tiny its name overshadows the depiction of its land mass on most maps, has come out of tragedy and now stands as an example of self-reliance and self-determination—a model that can and should be studied and perhaps applied in other nations, particularly as democratic movements have swept North Africa and the Middle East.

To the naysayers and disbelievers we would counter, "This is Rwanda. Expect more."

1

RWANDA NOW

The Skyscraper and the Chicken

The pace of change in Rwanda is a steady beat, the rhythm of a country on the move. Since its horrific genocide 18 years ago, in which a million or more people were killed in 100 days, Rwanda has completely reinvented itself. It has transformed from a nation divided by ethnic distinctions imposed by European colonizers to a nation where reconciliation and unification are powerful prerequisites for maintaining stability and achieving progress. Rwandans are coming together, united by the country's ambitious goal: to rise from crushing postgenocide poverty levels to become a middle-income country.

Evidence of Rwanda's recent achievements is everywhere, in its bricks-and-mortar, paved roads, and even fiber optics. Committed to evolving its economic foundation from subsistence agriculture to information and communications technology (ICT), the Rwandan government has invested $95 million to construct a 2,300-kilometer telecommunications network across the country, which is also linked to undersea cables along the East African coast. The network vastly improves broadband to attract electronic commerce and business process outsourcing. Connectivity isn't just for business, however. Along a rural road, a woman with a basket on her head or a man balancing bunches of bananas on the back of a bicycle he is pushing up a steep hill are probably also toting cell phones; according to government figures, 45.2 percent of the population had them in 2011, compared to just over 6 percent in 2006.

Of all these measures of progress, the most impressive is in poverty reduction. With overall real GDP growth in 2010–2011 of 8.2 percent, the country has reduced the percentage of its population living in poverty to 44.9 percent in 2011, from 56.9 percent in 2006. That translates into 1 million people, out of a total population of about 10.7 million, emerging from poverty in just five years. In addition, the number of people living in extreme poverty fell to 24 percent from 37 percent over the same period. Perhaps the even better news, and reflective of Rwanda's drive to raise the bottom of the socioeconomic pyramid, is that the so-called Gini coefficient, which measures inequality in distribution, showed decreases in income inequality, dropping to 0.49 from 0.52. In other words, Rwanda's programs to raise per capita income to about $560 today from $200 in 2000 (with a target of about $1,100 in per capita income by 2020) are not just benefiting the top; they're helping all Rwandans. Moreover, Rwanda is one of the few African countries that is on track to achieve most of its United Nations Millennium Development Goals, or MDGs—which target poverty reduction and improvements in education, health, and maternal/infant mortality—by 2015.

The magnitude of the turnaround, socially and economically, is sometimes referred to as a "miracle." Finance Minister John Rwangombwa, in an editorial for the *Wall Street Journal,* countered that notion when he wrote that there is "nothing supernatural about what we have achieved to date," which is but a "mere fraction of the ambitions we hold for our country. We understand that our accomplishments are the result of unrelenting focus by our country's leaders and citizens on getting the fundamentals right: government accountability and transparency, policies that attract trade and investment, a healthy and educated population."[1]

Although Rwanda is not yet where it wants to be, and must maintain and even accelerate its momentum of growth, it has already come an incredible distance in such a short time. Self-determination and self-reliance propel this nation forward, making it the ultimate turnaround story on a continent better known for broken promises and unfulfilled potential.

For many first-time Western visitors, what is often most striking about Rwanda is how clean it is: there is almost no litter anywhere. The second is how safe it is. An American woman who now lives in Kigali shared with us that, unlike other places in Africa, she does not think twice about walking alone at night carrying her laptop and cell phone; neither person nor property is at risk. The main reason is the highly visible presence of police and military. Soldiers in trucks en route to their stations or toting AK-47s on a street corner near a hotel frequented by foreigners are constant reminders of the importance of security and stability in a country that has known unspeakable brutality and still faces outside threats from former *genocidaires,* who were behind the 1994 genocide, and their supporters, some of whom have taken refuge across the border in eastern Congo.

Safety in Rwanda, however, is not defined only by its streets. It means that all its people, particularly the rural poor, face fewer risks thanks to achievements like compulsory education, universal health care, improved longevity, reduced maternal and infant mortality, and food security.

In our time in Kigali, we absorbed many other images of Rwanda's transformative journey and the vision behind it. Two in particular became indelible, a mix of past and present reminders: leaning forward toward the future with the knowledge that slipping backward is simply not an option. One is a skyscraper, a symbol of Rwanda's aspirations as a hub of business and technology. The other is a chicken, a reminder of the continued importance of raising the standard of living in a country where 80 percent of the population still exists as subsistence farmers on tiny plots of land.

First, the skyscraper. The 20-story Kigali City Tower, built by Rwandan businessman and investor Hatari Sekoko, punctuates the skyline of the capital city. On one of our trips to Rwanda in early 2011, the tower was under construction without an anchor tenant, a venture that would be unheard of in the United States, where a project of that scale could not be undertaken without at least one firm commitment. By early 2012, though, the tower was open for business and fully leased after Visa Inc., the global financial giant that had just launched a venture in Rwanda, took the last space. The boldness of constructing a tower of mixed-use office and retail space is part of the country's "if you build it, they will come" mentality. Like the skyscraper that rose where none was before, Rwanda is creating an entirely new present and future for itself through sheer determination and intention.

In our conversations with Rwandan President Paul Kagame, the theme of creating "something out of nothing" was raised repeatedly. "It's not about re-creation of what used to be, but creation of something that is actually very different—and from nothing," Kagame explained to us during an interview at the presidential offices. "It is a story that continues to this day."

Kagame makes a distinct impression as the architect and driver of the new Rwanda. Tall and pencil-slim, with eyeglasses and a thin mustache and a hint of beard, he has the serious look of a schoolmaster. Yet he also projects an iron will and a steely resolve. The attributes others assign to him—disciplined, organized, serious, forward-looking—are apparent within the first moments of meeting him. He also has a warm and engaging side and a subtle sense of humor. His accessibility as he greeted us was disarming, and the matter-of-fact way he spoke and welcomed questions broadcasted authenticity.

The president left another impression as well, which was confirmed in subsequent interviews and conversations with Rwandans, Americans, and Europeans. When looking at Rwanda now in contrast to where it has been, one person has clearly made the difference: President Kagame. Inside the country and out, Kagame is widely credited with orchestrating the turnaround of this devastated nation. He has been called a "visionary leader" by former UK Prime Minister Tony Blair and was presented with the Clinton Global Citizen Award by former U.S. President Bill Clinton in 2009. That same year he was named one of *Time* magazine's 100 Most Influential People.

"I think he's an outstanding leader because he has the unusual combination of a strong sense of vision and a practical desire to get the job done," Blair told us.

Blair has a real affection for Africa. During his term as British prime minister, he created a Department for International Development; Rwanda was one of the countries the department worked with early on. After leaving office, Blair founded the Africa Governance Initiative to support the development of governance and implementation skills in Africa, which he sees as critical for the future of the continent. Today, Blair's governance initiative is working closely with the Rwandan government to train its next generation of public servants.

As much as Rwanda strives toward the future, however, it has not forgotten its agrarian roots. This is where the chicken comes in. Fresh from the butcher in its brown and black feathers, the chicken was held by the feet by a smartly dressed woman in a bright print blouse, a slim blue skirt, and red high-heeled shoes. Watching the woman pick her way along an unpaved back street in Kigali, where the red earth had been scarred deeply by rains earlier in the season, we could only wonder where she was going with the bird: perhaps to her home or to a friend or relative who would undertake the plucking and cooking; maybe even to a restaurant she owned. Wherever the chicken was headed, it reminded us of the basics: while Rwanda steams ahead toward its vision of becoming a middle-income country on par with Singapore, it must also ensure the basic needs of its people are met: health care, education, and, of course, food. It was not so long ago, in the years before the genocide, that Rwanda knew famine in some of its regions. Only recently, in 2009, did the country achieve food security. Although in remote villages protein is still at a premium, nutrition programs, such as the government's initiative to give cows to poor families, are working to solve the problem.

In order for Rwanda to continue to feed itself and improve its economy, it must continue to develop its agricultural sector, which accounts for more than a third of that economy. Agriculture must become more mechanized, and tiny individual plots of land must be joined together in cooperatives to reap economies of scale on inputs such as fertilizer and seed, as well as cultivation and harvesting. In addition to staples such as beans and sorghum, Rwandan agriculture continues to emphasize crops such as coffee and tea for export, which reap badly needed foreign exchange. The country is always investigating new export crops.

Together, the skyscraper and the chicken spoke to us of progress to be made at both ends of the socioeconomic scale. It is not enough to elevate the top with new hotels and paved roads, foreign direct investment, and California-style houses in the hills around Kigali. The bottom of the pyramid must also climb upward through intensive and integrated efforts across the social, economic, and political spectrum.

"This country is run in a way that's efficient and focused on outcomes and delivery," said Dr. Paul Farmer, a renowned expert in global health issues at Harvard Medical School and cofounder of Partners In Health, which works closely with the Clinton Foundation and the Rwandan Ministry of Health to advance initiatives such as expanding access to HIV/AIDS treatment across the country and improving the number and quality of health facilities in rural areas. "It's quite clear that from the early years—even back in the 1990s, when he was not president—that President Kagame recognized inequality as a chief pathology in the country."

Rwanda has laid a foundation for its future where none existed before, from compulsory education for all children that was recently expanded from 9 years to 12, to embracing and enforcing a culture with zero tolerance for corruption, and decentralizing government to accord more responsibility and accountability at the local level. As part of the transformation, Rwanda has changed its official language from French to English, the *lingua franca* of business and technology. If you wonder just how far Rwanda will go to anchor itself in the modern global economy, consider the six-year-old child in a rural village who shakes your hand and asks in well-practiced English, "Hello, what is your name? What is your job?" She may be tomorrow's teacher, doctor, engineer, entrepreneur, or business leader. Most importantly, she is being raised without the ethnic identification that once so bitterly divided this nation between the majority Hutu and the minority Tutsi.

In our conversations, President Kagame shared with us his vision of all Rwandans as one people with common ancestry who must work together to realize the goals of a self-sufficient nation able to chart its own course in the world. "What is always on my mind is where we are going to be as a country and as a people in 10 or 20 years," he told us. "The other thing [I think about] is how I am going to make sure that everybody contributes tomorrow and the day after, so that they are the ones to do it and they are the ones to benefit. How do I make them realize what needs to be done, and what is in their best interest?"

During our meetings at the presidential offices, which were simply decorated and unimposing, Kagame demonstrated his passion for private-sector development, free markets, and capitalism, which have earned him comparisons to a corporate CEO. Indeed, we found he has more in common with the typical American executive than most political leaders, particularly in developing nations. And given what Rwanda has achieved in its turnaround, Kagame has proven himself to be a profound leader, particularly on a continent where positions of power and authority have too often been exploitative and damaging to the people.

But make no mistake, Rwanda is not perfect. This is no Garden of Eden for business where an investment today multiplies tenfold by tomorrow. The wheels turn slowly at times, to the frustration of some foreign investors, because of unnecessary bureaucracy and a lack of experience and confidence within the public sector. Patience, one foreign investor told us, is the name of the game in doing business in Rwanda. The development of human capital is a significant challenge, particularly at the middle tier. As a landlocked country, transportation costs are considerable, according to some estimates amounting to some 40 percent of the cost of imported retail goods. And Rwanda's heavy dependence on imported energy and lack of electrical distribution are major concerns. At the end of 2011, less than 11 percent of the households in Rwanda were electrified, although that percentage was still 2.5 times the electrification rate in 2006.

"Rwanda, like any nation, is not an impeccable place. It has many challenges and obstacles to overcome," commented Donald Kaberuka, president of the African Development Bank, who also served as Rwanda's minister of Finance and Economic Planning from 1997 through 2005 and is credited with helping stabilize the country's economy after the genocide. He cited the need for a diversified export base, lower energy costs, depth in the financial sector, and more foreign investment along with continued reconciliation and leadership development at all levels. "But Rwanda's track record to date gives her and her friends conviction that a prosperous nation, at peace with herself, connected into global networks of trade and capital, is feasible," he added.

Of all that has been achieved under Kagame's leadership, one of the most significant moments is yet to come, in 2017, when he is expected to step down from the presidency having served two seven-year, democratically elected terms. For Kagame, a seamless succession through democratic election is what will truly underscore his triumph, silencing critics and naysayers who have repeatedly speculated about a third term, which would require a change to Rwanda's constitution. For all that Rwanda has accomplished, the country continues to be a lightning rod for criticism. One of the most serious allegations is that Kagame stifled political opposition during the 2010 election, in which he was reelected with 93 percent of the vote, a landslide number that raised questions about its validity. Human rights activists in the West complain about a lack of political expression in the country after some political opponents were jailed for allegedly stirring up old ethnic tensions. After the Rwandan election, the White House expressed its concerns about "a series of disturbing events prior to the election," although it also acknowledged the "enormous challenges [in Rwanda] born of the genocide."[2] The Kagame administration, meanwhile, has defended its actions, maintaining that any promotion of genocide ideology will not be tolerated.

Ambassador Susan Rice, the U.S. permanent representative to the United Nations, delivered a speech in Kigali in November 2011 that lauded Rwanda's "remarkable progress . . . made against all odds," but also described the political culture of the country as "comparatively closed," based on what she called restrictions on the press and fears among activists, journalists, and political opponents about speaking out. "The deepening and broadening of democracy can be the next great achievement of this great country and its remarkable people," she added. "In Rwanda, economic development and political openness should reinforce each other. This is Rwanda's next developmental challenge."[3]

Whatever its challenges, Rwanda appears to be on track to make significant and sustainable progress economically, socially, and politically. Every sector and facet, from education to health, governance to private sector development, is in transition. Change is happening everywhere, concurrently and in a way that is purposefully interconnected. An ICT economy cannot happen without improvements in education. Education needs strong, stable communities. Stability requires reconciliation to continue the healing on the community and individual level, between perpetrator and victim and the children of each. Stability is enhanced by a sense of well-being, with access to health care and programs that improve the ability of families to feed themselves. It is a virtuous circle that cannot be broken or the entire cycle will be disrupted, which could threaten Rwanda's stability and reignite old tensions below the surface.

The Rwandan drama continues to play out on the world stage, where the current focus is sometimes sharply on the negative. In spite of the scrutiny—some of it perhaps deserved for a democracy-in-the-making, some clearly exaggerated—Rwanda remains focused on its goals of self-determination and a more secure and prosperous future. Every solution, every strategy put in place will be distinctly Rwandan. No matter what the outside world says, the perspective that matters most to Rwanda is how it sees itself.

A NEW CHAPTER IN RWANDA'S STORY

There is another revitalization going on in Rwanda that is no less important than any other aspect: the arts. In a country that admittedly puts much of its focus on doctors, engineers, and technicians trained in practical vocations, artists are finding their voices. In the Uburanga and Ivuka Arts galleries in Kigali, artists produce uniquely vibrant abstracts that draw from Rwandan life. In Rwanda, where there is no funding for art education and no publicly supported expositions, the blossoming of the art community is happening organically. It is an important development for a country as it moves beyond the basics. Indeed, many people judge a country by the quality of its arts; in Rwanda, the galleries are powerful incubators of possibilities.

At Ivuka on Saturday mornings, young boys beat tall standing drums and chant songs in Kinyarwanda, while young girls in T-shirts and flip-flops practice traditional Rwandan dances. In cooperatives across the country, women weave papyrus and other grasses into beautiful baskets that not only earn tourist dollars but, more importantly, preserve the country's cultural heritage. At a reception at a trendy new nightclub in Kigali, fashion designer Nicole Miller unveiled a partnership with Indego Africa, a cooperative of Rwandan women, to make fair-trade clothing and accessories and to teach the artisans advanced sewing and tailoring. The artistic community is a reminder that Rwanda is a multifaceted place that cannot be viewed only through one lens. In order to understand Rwanda, one must comprehend three time frames or "chapters" of its narrative. We asked Minister of Foreign Affairs and Cooperation Louise Mushikiwabo to elaborate. Well-spoken and elegantly dressed, "Minister Louise," as she is called, was raised in Rwanda but moved to the United States in 1986 and graduated from the University of Delaware in 1990. As tensions in Rwanda mounted, she stayed in the United States and worked in the Washington, DC, area for lobbying firms and later for the African Development Bank, a post that eventually took her to Tunisia. Then, in 2008, she received an invitation to join the Rwandan government, first as minister for information and then in foreign affairs. An author who has written widely on the subjects related to the Rwandan experience, Mushikiwabo presented the country's narrative as an unfolding story.

Chapter One dates back to "the struggle," the civil war that broke out in 1990, and extends through the genocide that raged in the country from April to July 1994, and through subsequent years of fighting to put down insurgencies and stabilize the country. Chapter Two began in 2000, with reconstruction and rebirth that lasted roughly a decade. Now, Rwanda is in the early stages of Chapter Three, a period of consolidating past experiences and building upon the new foundation of governance and economic development. "It is our national ambition now, and part of the policy of this ministry, to have a presence in the world. We want to define ourselves and to interact and open up as much as we can; to bring to Rwanda opportunities from the world, whether in trade or know-how or good practices—those things that allow Rwandans to have a better life and that will raise the standard of life for Rwanda," Mushikiwabo commented. "That is what Chapter Three is."

Rwanda's Chapter Three also carries a sobering theme: what has been accomplished thus far must be surpassed. Economically, the current GDP growth rate of 7 to 8 percent must expand even faster if Rwanda is to continue to significantly reduce poverty. Lifting up more people will require jobs, which, in turn, means greater economic development. Rwanda has become a force within the East African Community—which also includes Kenya, Uganda, Burundi, and Tanzania—to pursue economic and trade integration, and eventually a common currency. On the broader international scene, Rwanda has signed a bilateral trade agreement with the United States and publicly mended diplomatic fences with its former nemesis, France, which had supported the government regime behind the genocide.

It is not enough for Rwanda to keep doing what it has done; it must do more in order to leapfrog to where it wants to be. Not surprising, Kagame and his team of ministers believe it is possible. "I have confidence that we will do even better than 8.2 percent average [GDP growth] in the next five years," Finance Minister Rwangombwa told us. "We have a stronger base in terms of capacity and infrastructure and our legal system. And the world knows Rwanda better now than in the last five years."

The world knowing Rwanda means moving beyond being defined only by the genocide (a story repeated perhaps too often in the donor community in an effort to raise funds), and to become recognized for its potential for foreign direct investment. One obvious area is tourism, which currently brings in 50 percent of all foreign exchange into the country. Many visitors come to Rwanda to see the mountain gorillas known as "silverbacks," the endangered animals studied by famed naturalist Dian Fossey, who was credited with saving these animals from poachers until she was murdered in 1985. The country also has national parks, including the wildlife refuge at Akagera where lions and black rhinos are being reintroduced, as well as the considerable natural beauty of its lakes and hills. As a result, hotel construction is booming, bringing in such major brands as Marriott and Radisson.

But Rwanda must also educate and train its young workforce, and equip them with the technical and customer-service skills valued by foreign companies that Rwanda hopes will set up operations in the country. Rwanda has already attracted foreign investment. The Chinese are there, having built roads, office buildings, and a large hotel; the South Africans are there with a large telecommunications presence, just to name two. Many more are being courted. Development of a homegrown private sector of small and midsized companies will attract the next generation of Rwandan-born entrepreneurs.

In its *Doing Business 2012* report, the World Bank ranked Rwanda number 45 in the world for ease of doing business, up from 50 the year before, in recognition of strides such as reducing business registration fees, improving credit information, and decreasing the frequency of value-added tax filings by companies from monthly to quarterly. Rwanda has taken a "broad approach to making business regulation business-friendly," the World Bank report stated. "The economy has undertaken ambitious land and judicial reforms, often years in the making. Since 2001, Rwanda has introduced new corporate, insolvency, civil procedure, and secured transaction laws. And it has streamlined and remodeled institutions and processes for starting a business, registering property, trading across borders and enforcing a contract through the courts."[4]

Also positive for the business climate has been Rwanda's success in curbing inflation, particularly when compared with its East African neighbors. According to a January 2012 report in

African Business magazine, Rwanda's inflation rate was between 8 and 8.7 percent in 2011, which is attributable to improved co-ordination between fiscal and monetary policy. By comparison, inflation in Uganda hit 28.3 percent in September 2011, while in Kenya it reached 17.3 percent. "Even though Rwanda, like the rest of Africa, is faced with an unstable and turbulent global economy, it has managed to produce a sound economic performance," the article added.[5]

Perhaps the most unique and distinguishing characteristic in Rwanda is the government's zero tolerance for corruption. On a continent where wealth all too often ends up in the pockets of the elite, and where doing even basic business involves red tape and money to grease the wheels, Rwanda is a startling exception. Although Kagame has shunned the idea that corruption is an African problem, foreign investors compare Rwanda favorably to places such as Nigeria, whose notorious corruption problem has inhibited the ability of many foreign companies to set up shop there, and also Kenya and South Africa, where corruption has become a growing menace in recent years. In our conversations with consultants, entrepreneurs, and Rwandan and foreign business investors, Rwanda's zero tolerance for corruption topped the list of reasons for doing business in the country.

"In Rwanda, you have a stable democracy and good governance," observed Clifford Sacks, CEO for Africa and Head of Pan-African Equities for Renaissance Capital, an emerging-markets investment bank. "Those are massive tailwinds for the country."

Rwanda's success, ultimately, will depend on how well it can maximize its potential for foreign investment, which will require some big names, particularly in the ICT sector. "When you are not endowed with oil and all these other natural resources, you can use technology and innovation together to achieve economic goals," Foreign Affairs Minister Mushikiwabo remarked. "We are determined to become a service economy. We need to professionalize and we need to do it fast." As Kagame also observed, "We have to focus on our own major resource, which is our people."

To an outsider, the goals of this tiny, landlocked country might seem lofty, to say the least. "But what choice does Rwanda have?" the government remarked in the country's Vision 2020, a sweeping plan for economic, social, and political development that was drafted in 2000. "To remain in the current situation is simply unacceptable for the Rwandan people."[6] Rwanda's only way forward is to embrace a development plan and generate the resources necessary to achieve it. If other comparable countries, particularly in East Asia, have turned dreams of economic development into reality, then why not Rwanda? What it must do now is execute its plans in order to turn dreams into realities, thus creating opportunities for its people, particularly the new generation of professionals who are seeking jobs that do not yet exist. As the recent democratic uprisings in North Africa and the Arab world illustrate, woe to the country with an educated population and high unemployment; this is a problem Rwanda is committed to avoiding at all costs.

Can Rwanda succeed? Will it manage to reduce poverty, improve education and health care, expand the private sector, encourage foreign investment, support stability and security, develop institutions, and continue on the path of developing full democracy? Will it realize the promise of the skyscraper while still minding the chickens, those basic needs that make a huge impact on the population at the bottom of the socioeconomic scale?

Based upon our conversations with people across the economy, we think it highly likely. As we will explore in upcoming chapters, Rwanda has a robust plan of execution to address its challenges and opportunities. Moreover, given where it has been—in the pit of despair and destruction—and how far it has come in less than two decades, there is no reason to doubt the country's resolve. With the strength of its leadership to drive execution, Rwanda may indeed rise faster and farther than anyone expects.

2

A NATION DIVIDED BY HATRED AND HORROR

A contemplative walkway winds around the grounds of the Kigali Memorial Centre, through gardens and underneath an arbor covered by a blossoming vine. From the path, a visitor can look out toward the hills of Kigali, where very modest dwellings cluster along the sides and multistory buildings and a lone skyscraper crown the top. What that panorama does not show, however, is the Kigali of less than two decades ago, when dead and decomposing bodies littered the streets, and ravenous dogs fed on corpses. Faced with the current scene of promising and hopeful activity, it seems incomprehensible.

To imagine the horror of what was, one needs to turn in the other direction, toward the white building with the peaked roofline and wide windows. Here, in the Kigali Memorial Centre, Rwanda has memorialized its tragic, unspeakable past, a genocide that from April to July 1994 saw as many as one million people (and quite possibly more) murdered by bands of government-sanctioned militias that incited violence and urged one group to kill another. In the midst of the terror, another two million people fled the country, which today has a population of 10.7 million. The objective of the *genocidaires* was clear: to eradicate the minority Tutsi at the hands of the majority Hutu.

Some 250,000 of the dead are buried at the memorial center, in mass graves that are decorated on any given day with bouquets of calla lilies, roses, and carnations. Wrapped in plastic and tied with white ribbons, many bear banners that read "never forget." In Rwanda, the dead will never be forgotten; everyone has a story of at least one friend or relative. Even in the midst of forward progress, the ghost of what happened here—unfathomable, and within the lifetime of the country's many young adults—is a constant reminder.

The genocide is deeply embedded in the narrative of the country. People opened up to us with at least pieces of their stories: what they saw, what happened to family members, what they endured. They often related these with a tone of acceptance: the past is past. Now, reconciliation and unification are preached everywhere, politically and spiritually.

Another big part of the genocide story is that of a country abandoned by the West. As Americans, it was uncomfortable for us to be reminded of how the United States, having suffered defeat and embarrassment in Somalia and afraid of getting entangled in another prolonged, Bosnia-like battle, did nothing to stop the genocide. The United Nations tied its own hands, sending a paltry and impotent force that was supposed to keep the peace but could do virtually nothing to intervene, even as people were hacked to death by machete while UN soldiers looked on in horror. There is Rwandan blood on so many hands.

The violence began in April 1994, when the former president of Rwanda, Juvénal Habyarimana, was killed when his plane was mysteriously shot down. However, treating the genocide as if it were the result of one incident is grossly inaccurate. Genocide, as the Kigali Memorial Centre reminds visitors, is never spontaneous. It is an intentional act.

Gérard Prunier, a researcher and historian, called the Rwandan genocide a "historical product, not a biological fatality or a 'spontaneous' bestial outburst." Rather, as he wrote in his book *The Rwanda Crisis: History of a Genocide*, "The Rwandese genocide is the result of a process which must be analyzed." It is beyond the scope of these pages to give an in-depth analysis of the genocide, which was the result of complex rivalries and relationships among two groups that had formerly coexisted as socioeconomic classes: the Tutsi, who raised cattle, and the Hutu, who farmed the land. A third group, making up only one percent of the population, was the Twa, who tended to be small in stature and descended from Pygmy ancestry. As Prunier observed, the first European explorers to reach Rwanda in the late 1800s misidentified the three groups as tribes, even though they shared the same language and culture and lived side by side, not separated in any way. [1]

There was intermarriage among Hutu and Tutsi, as well as common cultural aspects such as religion. (Prunier notes that, in precolonial Rwandan society, Hutu endowed with cattle could, in effect, be considered Tutsi.) This complex society, governed by a hierarchical structure of a mwami (king) and layers of chiefs and subchiefs, was completely misinterpreted and manipulated with racist theories promulgated by Belgian colonizers. The Belgians, who took over the Rwandan territory after Germany's defeat in World War I, decided erroneously that the Tutsi were not African at all, but a race of Caucasian origin and therefore superior to the Hutu. By 1933, the Belgians had begun requiring all Rwandans to carry identity cards marked Hutu or Tutsi. Those same cards would later become the scourge of the country, cleaving one people into two and stoking fires of enmity between them.

The Belgians aligned themselves at first with the Tutsi, establishing them as the country's aristocracy to rule over the Hutu. In time, though, the concept of a minority ruling over the majority chafed some of the Belgian priests who had been dispatched by the Catholic Church to tend to the Rwandan flock of faithful. Given their own political and social backgrounds, the White Fathers, as they were called, identified with the oppressed and decided that rule by Tutsi minority over the Hutu majority must come to an end. As Stephen Kinzer observed in his book, *A Thousand Hills,* "Many [of the clerics] were Flemish, meaning that they had humble backgrounds, came from a group that considered itself victimized and even oppressed by other Belgians, and sympathized with socialism." Under the influence of the Catholic clergy, the Belgian officials began to plot a new ruling system for Rwanda, one that would supposedly be more democratic.[2] This required a new alignment with the Hutu while abandoning former Tutsi allies. Then came the Hutu Manifesto in 1957, an incendiary document that encouraged the Hutu to throw off the domination of the Tutsi. Grégoire Kayibanda formed the Movement for Hutu Liberation (PARMEHUTU), calling for a new system under which Hutu would rule and Tutsi would be subservient.

As the Belgians tried to manage the Rwandan transition to independence under Hutu rule, the Rwandan monarch, King Mutara III Rudahigwa, who ruled from 1931 to 1959, strongly opposed it. His opposition, however, was short-lived. As Kinzer relates, "Belgian officials invited him to neighboring Burundi to discuss their differences. He arrived on July 25, 1959, and after taking a few bites of lunch his hosts had prepared for him, he fell ill. He was brought to a Belgian doctor but quickly died. Many Rwandans quickly concluded that the mwami's death was another Belgian crime. Whatever the truth, his passing removed the most visible opponent of Belgian policy and the Hutu militancy it encouraged."[3]

As the campaign for Hutu rule gathered steam, Tutsi went from being the aristocracy, enjoying the favor of colonizers, to being hunted, expelled, and murdered. The first pogroms against the Tutsi began in 1959. An estimated 130,000 to 150,000 Tutsi fled Rwanda in the first waves of violence in the early 1960s, in which as many as 20,000 people were killed. One of the near victims was a very young Paul Kagame, who was born in October 1957. His childhood and early adult years would completely coincide with Rwanda's history of expulsion, exile, civil war, and, later, genocide.

Sitting in the presidential offices, he recalled the story, his earliest memory. Tellingly, he never used the labels "Tutsi" or "Hutu," nor did he ever self-identify as Tutsi. Rather, he told the story as a Rwandan who shares in the bitter history of all his people.

"The pictures stay with me," Kagame told us. "There were killings and burning of homes, slaughtering of cattle all over the place, and smoke from all the houses burning down." Such scenes, which must have been frightening and confusing to a little boy, were easily visible from the family home, atop a hill which looked out onto a valley and then up the side of another hill.

His father was away at the time, having fled out of fear he would be killed; he went first to Burundi, then crossed into Congo and finally to Uganda. His mother, Asteria, knew what was coming and told her children the truth: they would be killed. She gathered the children who were with her at the time, including Paul, his brother (who would later die in 1985 in the war in Uganda), and their sisters. Not wanting them to be killed inside the home, Asteria led her children into the compound to wait; there was no plan to hide, no reason to expect they could escape. Suddenly, a vehicle appeared that Asteria recognized: a chauffeured car from the royal palace, sent by one of her relatives. As they were shepherded into the car, young Kagame heard traditional cow-horn trumpets being blown, a warning that the family was leaving. Before the killers could make it across the valley and up the hill, Kagame and his family had escaped.

Although the incident is vital to his personal story, Kagame told it as part of a broader narrative. It is important to understand, Kagame told us, that the seeds of the genocide in 1994 were sown many years before by colonizers and church leaders.

From his formative years on, Kagame's personal story was one of exile, of living as a refugee like so many other displaced Rwandans throughout East Africa. Many were in Uganda, where Kagame's family settled. Life there was hard, and they were constantly reminded that they were outsiders, unwelcome. "We were leading a refugee life. It was totally in contradiction to the life we were used to before," he recalled. "The life of my family, my parents, before this happened was very decent in terms of the standard for Rwandans then." Instead of having their own home and landholdings, Kagame's family was reduced to living in refugee camps, sometimes in a tent. Yet even that kind of harsh life, he recalled, did not "break their desire to uphold themselves to a certain level, a dignified level." No matter how basic or modest, their home was clean and organized, a reflection of his parents' disciplinarian nature. In our conversations with many people about Kagame's leadership today, the word *disciplined* is mentioned every time.

Looking back, Kagame spoke with admiration for his mother, whom he called "more resilient than my father, in a sense." His father, whom he described as brooding and constantly chain-smoking, had difficulty accepting the change in his circumstances. Yet no matter where the family went, his father, a former entrepreneur who had been an owner of what became the TRAFIPRO coffee cooperative, always emerged as a leader among the refugees, speaking out on their behalf and helping mediate internal problems. His mother, however, did something she had never been trained to do: she picked up a hoe and began clearing the bush and cultivating crops to feed her family. "My mother concentrated on how we would live by doing things she never knew how to do, like tilling the ground and growing crops that would provide food for us," Kagame explained. "In other words, we grew more or less dependent on our mother—including our father, who rejected [the work] saying, 'I can't do it. I have never done it and I don't want to do it.'"

As Kagame spoke, it became obvious what traits he had inherited, whether by nature or nurture, from his parents. He is both highly resilient, like his mother, and a natural-born leader like his father. Kagame's most apparent departure from his father is his lack of brooding. Indeed, Kagame's early memories of refugee life in Uganda were interspersed with a sense of lightheartedness; for example, sitting with his peers under a tree and learning his lessons with only a stick with which to "write" by scratching on his legs. "Then we would go to the teacher to mark us. It was fun and we enjoyed it," he recalled. Later, when there was a little money to buy a ballpoint pen, Kagame used a freshly picked banana leaf as his notebook. He and his peers enjoyed games of football (soccer), of which he remains a passionate fan. "We enjoyed our life, even though it wasn't really normal life," he told us.

By the late 1960s, however, Kagame began questioning why the family was living as refugees outside Rwanda, the place he remembered as home, and why they were not welcomed by the Ugandans around them. "I asked them, 'Did we do something wrong to deserve this, to be here?' I realized that we were supposed to be in Rwanda and be better off. [I recalled] when we almost got killed and had to flee. I wanted to know, 'Was that it? Is that the reason why we left?'"

His parents then began telling stories of Rwanda and its history, of the roles played by the Belgian colonizers and the Catholic Church, of "the conspiracies that went on and how the whole social fabric was torn apart in our country and the underlying causes," Kagame explained. Yet Kagame, like so many of the people we spoke to who grew up as refugees in other countries, never stopped seeing himself as Rwandan. Even later, when he became an officer in the Ugandan army and then a valued member of the military force that helped to overthrown a dictatorship in that country, Kagame was, first and foremost, a Rwandan.

For him, as for so many others, Rwanda was kept alive with stories, as both a legacy and as an ancestral home to which they would all return one day. During their exile, the radio was their link to that home.

Kagame and his brother tuned the family's small FM radio to Rwandan broadcasts, which enabled them to hear stories in Kinyarwanda, the native language of their home country, as well as bits of folklore and wisdom. One program, called *Did You Know*, shared helpful hints such as the medicinal use of a plant that grows wild in untended gardens. The leaves of the plant can be crushed and put on a wound to fight infection and promote healing. Years later, while fighting in Uganda and then in the bush against Rwandan government forces, Kagame would remember and literally apply that lesson.

As time went on, Kagame felt drawn back to Rwanda. But first, duty called in his adopted home of Uganda, a country with a tumultuous political history. It was led in its early years of independence in the 1960s by Milton Obote, who was toppled in a coup in 1971 by the infamous dictator Idi Amin. In 1979, the Tanzanian army invaded the country and, together with a Ugandan liberating force, successfully ousted Amin, who fled the country. Two subsequent leaders came to power before Obote returned as president in 1980. In 1985, Obote was deposed in another coup and replaced by Tito Okello. During this time, Kagame and another young Rwandan serving in the Ugandan army, his best friend Fred Rwigema, joined forces with Yoweri Museveni, a Ugandan reformer who preached an ideology of reform with Marxist overtones and believed that Africa should be ruled by Africans. As members of the Ugandan National Resistance Army, Kagame and Rwigema pledged to help overthrow the government in Uganda and bring Museveni to power. Later, while still serving in the Ugandan army, Kagame and Rwigema would collaborate on a secret plot of their own design: the liberation and unification of their own homeland. But first, there were battles to be fought and lessons to be learned in the Ugandan struggle.

"We were fighting injustice in Uganda," Kagame explained, recalling his service in the Ugandan army, in which he was elevated to the rank of major and made head of military intelligence. At the same time, there was injustice in Rwanda, the persecution of one group of people by another largely for the gain of the ruling elite in Habyarimana's regime, who kept the country shackled to European benefactors. The refugees also bore many hardships. Even as an officer in the Ugandan army, Kagame was acutely aware of the prejudice that existed against Rwandans, who were constantly reminded of their refugee status. "A flash would come to you that it was not your place. There was no need to be reminded. You would either see it or smell it or experience it," he recalled. "The refugee life, the struggle life, came together and solidified everything."

One of the Rwandan leaders who remembered Kagame well from these times in Uganda is General James Kabarebe. Tall, with a military bearing, Kabarebe has a commanding presence. Yet when he sat down with us in his office at the Ministry of Defense, he became an animated and engaging storyteller who recalled first meeting Kagame in the mid-1980s when both men were part of the Ugandan army. "Everybody held him in high esteem," Kabarebe said of Kagame, whom he described as demonstrating the same strictness, discipline, and attention to details then that he is praised for today. "He is consistent in his life,"

Kabarebe added. "Today, if I go to a meeting with him, watch him speak on TV or speak to the public, I can anticipate what he will say about anything, because he never deviates."

Kabarebe recalled an incident in which Kagame showed his unshakeable resolve. A "notorious Ugandan commander," in Kabarebe's words, with unmistakable contempt for Rwandan soldiers, had earned a reputation for mistreating Rwandans under his command. Fed up with the reports he was hearing, Kagame called the Ugandan commander into his office and was later seen holding the other man by the trousers as he pulled him down the steps outside, all the while chastising him for his treatment of the Rwandan recruits. "When I saw it I was very happy," Kabarebe recalled. "Normally, in those days, if you were Rwandan you were not privileged. You were a second-class nobody."

The Ugandan bush war ended in 1986, and Museveni became the new president. Kagame and Fred Rwigema continued as leaders in the Ugandan army: Rwigema became a major general and army chief of staff; Kagame commanded intelligence officers and later trained in Cuba on guerilla techniques. After the Cuban experience, Kagame and Rwigema seized upon their next mission, a covert operation to win back their country. They started from within the Ugandan army, enlisting the support of the Rwandans who served. In time, the group known as the Rwandan Patriotic Front (RPF) would become a global network of refugees, exiles, and their supporters.

FROM GRASSROOTS TO A GLOBAL NETWORK

Among those who joined the RPF early on was a young college student who had been born in Uganda and whose father had been killed in Rwanda before she was born. Petite and soft-spoken, there is nothing in her demeanor today that suggests a revolutionary streak. Yet to many, she is at the heart of the RPF, the one who undertook the incredible responsibility of helping raise funds for the fight to regain and unify the country.

Today, Aloisea Inyumba is minister of Gender and Family Promotion, having served previously as a senator in the Rwandan Parliament and, before that, as governor of Kigali-Ngali Province. She was also a former commissioner and executive secretary of Rwanda's Unity and Reconciliation Commission, overseeing the public debate over reconciliation. Immediately after the genocide, she was the first minister of Family, Gender, and Social Affairs. Among her duties postgenocide was overseeing burial of the dead, the resettlement of refugees, and a national campaign to adopt orphans.

Her early story echoed that of others: she grew up in a refugee camp in Uganda where the Rwandan culture was kept alive through traditions, language, music, and dance. She talked about her mother having a small radio that allowed them to hear Rwandan programs and songs. By the time Inyumba went to high school, she and her Rwandan classmates were urged to change their names and hide their true national identities. "If you saw someone wearing a traditional Rwandan dress, you would run away. You couldn't associate because people would say, 'This is a Rwandese.' We were always concealing our true identity," she recalled. "It was so painful."

Fortunately, Inyumba had a close friend who was Ugandan, whose father filled out high school registration forms on her behalf, claiming she was also his daughter. Later, she attended Makerere University in Uganda, where she received a degree in social work and social administration. It was during her time at university that Inyumba volunteered with the RPF, which was then an underground organization. "There was always that kind of feeling that we needed justice and a true home," she explained. "Those feelings were always with us. We knew that one day we would have to go home."

From the beginning, Inyumba recalled, women were part of the struggle, respected by their male counterparts in the RPF. In fact, the concept of a ministry-level organization to promote and protect the rights of women had been a founding principle of the RPF. "I never encountered any form of discrimination or abuse," she said, which she credited to Fred Rwigema and other leaders. Her first assignment was education, becoming a "trainer of trainers" immersed in the RPF cause of unifying the country for all Rwandans. Central to indoctrination in the RPF was "peace training," which preached a doctrine of love, fairness, and forgiveness, not based in any religion or denomination but rather drawing from elements of Rwandan culture and values. "You can't talk about Hutu and Tutsi and Twa. We are one," Inyumba recalled. "They would teach us about common ancestry."

For a young woman whose father had been killed because he was Tutsi, this radical thinking brought peace of mind. "It contributed to our daily reconciliation," she added. "We had always lived a lie. People had told us we were different. For the first time, in this [peace training] class, they were telling us we were Rwandan."

Reconciliation classes were essential to the RPF cause and reflective of the thinking and motivation of its leaders. The struggle was not for one group to oust or dominate the other, or to extract revenge for those who had been killed. Simply stated, RPF was never intended to be a Tutsi organization. Again and again, the message was that no difference existed among Rwandans. Kagame, she recalled, was particularly strong on reconciliation. "That is my measure in a leader: do they really understand that this is a country that belongs to all of us? We knew right from the beginning, they [RPF leaders] were committed to reconciliation," she remarked.

After serving in the Civic Education Department, Inyumba became director of production, organizing projects—such as making shoes and buttons and selling milk—to raise money. From there, she moved to the Finance Department, where she kept track of money with simplicity and transparency, which were also key RPF leadership principles. Reports were kept to one page so they could be easily understood and the chance for error or obfuscation eliminated: what was received, the amount spent, and the balance. Later, when the RPF waged war to retake the country, donations became more urgent. Monthly contributions came from supporters throughout the region—Uganda, Tanzania, Burundi, Kenya, and Congo—as well as from Canada, the United States, and Europe. When the war escalated, so did fundraising, always with a priority on the basics of medicine and food for an army that was outnumbered and ill-equipped. In the beginning, RPF soldiers wore jeans and street clothes; boots were at a premium. (Later, as East German factories were closing after the fall of the Berlin Wall in 1989, the RPF obtained uniforms at a very reasonable price.) In addition to money, fundraisers brought in maize (corn) and beans from the farmers' harvests, and occasionally trucks and cars. At one particular event, Inyumba recalled, ten vehicles were donated.

Traveling to Belgium for the first time to collect funds from supporters there, Inyumba wasn't sure what to expect. In the dead of winter, she walked in sandals without a coat, carrying a shopping bag of full of cash donations. Coincidentally, Paul Kagame was also in Brussels and spotted her on the street as he drove past. Stopping the car, he urged her to get inside. It never occurred to Inyumba to use a single franc in the collection for a taxi ride to where she was staying: the money was for the cause. "People knew we were accountable and were not going to cheat. We didn't take that [trust] for granted," she explained. "A number of our colleagues died, so we knew we had to be honest. For the sake of the lives that were lost, we had to be good people. Even today, that directs us to serve this country."

Among the other women in the RPF was Rose Kabuye, who later rose to the rank of major. Kabuye recalled the two leaders of the Rwandan cause: Fred Rwigema, who was outgoing and warm and enjoyed singing with the soldiers, and Paul Kagame, whose nature was very different: quiet, reserved, determined. Like Inyumba, Kabuye had been a student when she heard about the RPF and wanted to be recruited. Apparently unconvinced that this college girl with long hair was sincere about becoming a soldier, RPF organizers tried to discourage Kabuye at first by telling her she needed a recommendation. She went back to her university and contacted a sociology professor who provided her the necessary letter; with that she was welcomed into the RPF as a soldier.

Kabuye laughed heartily at herself as she recalled the rude awakening that greeted her and her friend Agnes when they were deployed for military training, toting their clothes along on hangers. In the jungle, the officers shaved Kabuye's head; she shed tears afterward in secret. Tall and slim, Kabuye quickly impressed her comrades during training that highlighted her natural athletic ability. When she went back to university for graduation ceremonies, Kabuye wore a wig to cover her shaved head. Yet even there, Kabuye was no longer a student, but a soldier, a commitment that would soon clash with her family life.

Kabuye married her husband, David, who was also recruited to the RPF. A year later, she had a baby boy, whose birth coincided with another momentous occasion. On October 1, 1990, when the baby was only one month old, the RPF launched its first incursion out of Uganda and into Rwanda to challenge the Habyarimana regime and unify the country. When Kabuye heard about it, she was furious at having been left behind. The quandary she faced obviously pained her even 22 years later, as she described deciding whether to leave her child in the care of others (first her husband, and then with relatives when he, too, joined the fight). Her mind made up, Kabuye immediately left for the front. "Sometimes people have to fight for their rights," reflected Kabuye, who later became mayor of Kigali immediately after the genocide and then served a seven-year term as Chief of Protocol in the Kagame administration. "Otherwise there would never be a Rwanda for us—no life, no home, nothing. This was a cause worth fighting for."

In the early days, the RPF troops were led by "Commander Fred" Rwigema. Kagame, meanwhile, had been sent by the Ugandan army for training at the U.S. Army Command and General Staff College at Fort Leavenworth, Kansas, one of the most sought after military training opportunities. During the four or five months Kagame was at staff college, he received invaluable training about tactics, strategy, and the history and causes of wars. Although he had moved to Kansas with his new wife, Jeannette, a young Rwandan woman who grew up in Nairobi, Kagame's mind was always on Rwanda and the RPF's secret plot to liberate and unify the country. He remained in close contact with Rwigema by telephone.

When the RPF launched its incursion into Rwanda, Kagame couldn't shake a nagging feeling that something was amiss. Reports by the BBC and the newspapers, as well as intelligence from contacts in Uganda and Belgium, suggested the ground fighting was sporadic and disorganized. He concluded that something must have gone terribly wrong. He contacted someone in Uganda with instructions to go look for Rwigema and come back with an answer. When his contact was blocked from seeing Rwigema, Kagame sent someone else back with a satellite phone and an explicit directive to call him from the field. When the call finally came in, Kagame demanded to know if his contact had seen Rwigema. "No, sir," he was told.

When Kagame asked why, his contact broke down on the telephone and began crying. "He's not there," the contact kept repeating in Kinyarwanda.

"Do you mean that he is dead?" Kagame asked.

"Yes," the contact said.

Kagame, who had already begun the process of leaving staff college, resolved to depart immediately, despite being in the middle of his studies. When he explained the situation to his superiors—that although he was being trained as part of the Ugandan army, he was a Rwandan who needed to join the fight to liberate his country—staff college leadership did not understand. "They thought something had gone nuts about me," Kagame told us. "They said, 'Are you sure you want to go?' I told them, 'I am dying to go . . . to fight for my country.'"

Convinced that Kagame was not going to change his mind, his superiors asked what they could do for him. "Can I take some of the books we are reading?" Kagame asked. Told he could take whatever books he wanted, Kagame left with the volumes he found most helpful, which he kept with him until they were lost in 1993.

On his way back to Rwanda, Kagame must have been confronted with both the sadness of the death of his best friend and the enormous task that lay before him. Rwigema had died on the second day of battle, but his death was kept secret from the troops and even his family for as long as possible, although rumors immediately began circulating. When Rose Kabuye arrived at the front, she was told in confidence that Rwigema had been killed but that his death could not be talked about with anyone. "No one was able to discuss what happened," she recalled. "The war went on as planned. People claimed that Fred was on the front lines, but after two weeks, we started to believe he was gone. We were paralyzed."

The fear was that once troops found out their leader was gone, they would become completely demoralized. "Then the enemy would start marauding us and killing us like grasshoppers," Defense Minister Kabarebe recalled. This disintegrating group was in dire need of a leader; the only hope was that Kagame was on his way.

In the interim, some RPF soldiers deserted; others threw themselves into the river to drown rather than be captured. In total confusion and despair, the RPF seemed to face imminent defeat. Into this mess came Kagame, who saw from the moment he arrived how desperately the troops needed both hope and discipline.

"People would look at him, at his face, to see if he was still strong," Kabarebe described. "There was nobody else in our struggle who could command that, who had that influence when everyone else was resigned, when the whole organization has disintegrated and everybody was running away. They were dying—physically and morally, hungry and wounded. It was a desperate situation. Only one individual could stand out and say, 'No, we will continue.'"

The situation that greeted Kagame just a few weeks into the war was so dire he could not help but ask himself why this burden had to fall on his shoulders. Why was he the one faced with this seemingly insurmountable challenge? "It wasn't clear that this was a solvable problem," he recalled. "It looked so confused, so complicated. It wasn't providing me with an opportunity to see where to start from."

Although clearly confident in his leadership abilities, Kagame described himself to us as being reluctant at times to step up and take the top role, to say, "I am the one to do this." Yet he also knew this was his responsibility, one he had to bear. His first decision as a leader was simply to take a stand, to not be destabilized by what was happening around him. "There was no alternative. There was absolutely none," he explained. "I communicated that with myself first, before I told anybody. [That resolve] stabilized me so I would not to be crushed under the weight of what I was facing."

Thus resolved, Kagame began talking to the troops, starting with those he could "bring back to the center," as he called it, and then to others who might also listen. His message, repeated over and over, was that leaving the Ugandan army and invading their homeland was not a process that could be reversed. Many of those in the RPF had faith in him, that somehow he could make the crucial difference. There were even those who believed that had he been there with them instead of training at the staff college at Leavenworth, the initial events of the war would have turned out differently. Looking back, however, and imagining what could have been was not helpful. The only option was to regroup and move forward.

"He has the courage to deal with very difficult situations," Kabarebe said of Kagame. "He stays strong and then others also gain some courage to stay strong, but not on their own. They stay strong leaning on him."

The image burned into Kabarebe's memory is of Kagame as a lone figure standing in the middle of the road, with the enemy approaching, dispatching the troops to safety. The final group to leave was the soldiers guarding where Fred Rwigema had been buried. Kabarebe got a good look at Commander Fred's resting place, and a particular tree growing nearby. Later, when it was time to exhume Rwigema's body and move it to Kigali for a hero's burial, that memory would play a critical part.

What remained of the RPF needed to be strengthened, disciplined, and turned into a well-trained guerilla fighting force. The decision took Kagame in a completely unexpected direction, to the north and the harsh conditions of the Virunga Mountains, a volcanic range that rises more than 10,000 feet and is home to the endangered mountain gorillas. While a smaller contingent remained close to the border with Uganda to distract government forces, a larger group went to Virunga. The elements kept them safe from the enemy—the Rwandan government forces—but cold and hunger would also take their toll.

Kabuye, meanwhile, was sent with the sick and wounded, but without doctors or medicine to treat them. She described a horrific scene of evacuating across a river: some made it by boat, while others jumped in the river and tried to swim; several drowned. Finally, she was able to secure medical assistance and money to buy medicine. After the first three weeks of triage, Kabuye decided to stay with the sick and wounded and help care for them.

For the fighters in Virunga, without proper clothing or enough food, suffering was a way of life, but the conditions hardened them in body and mind. Kagame in particular had an eerie ability to survive without much food or sleep, leading even those closest to him to wonder, "How does he do it?"

"We were always worried for his health," Minister of Gender Inyumba recalled. "Sometimes it was raining and kept drizzling. We would look at this man, sitting out in the rain, and wonder, 'Are we going to come out of this forest with this man who is not eating?'"

Kagame brought a new discipline to the RPF troops, with a code that established as capital offenses murder, rape, violent robbery, and desertion, and made punishable other offenses such as drinking alcohol, using drugs, failing to pay for goods, and promiscuous behavior. Troops who had lost all hope and sense of direction found a reason to believe, which for them was embodied in one person, one leader. What lay ahead was a plan to restore the country for all Rwandans. Although a peace accord would temporarily put an end to civil war, a more sinister force was brewing, one that would leave Rwanda devastated by a specter to haunt it forever: genocide. It would fall to Kagame and the RPF to stop the mass killings when the rest of the world turned a blind eye.

3

MARCHING INTO HELL

For the average newspaper reader, a report published in January 1991—about a battle in Ruhengeri in northern Rwanda, a skirmish in a place far off the map of Western consciousness—probably didn't register. The *Reuters* article, which appeared in the *New York Times,* simply stated that 400 to 600 rebels had fought against the Rwandan government's armed forces in Ruhengeri, close to the Ugandan border and the Virunga park that is home to the famed silverback gorillas. The rebels were not even identified by their name, the Rwandan Patriotic Front (RPF); instead, the article only mentioned that the fighters were from the same group that had invaded the country the previous October. This time, though, the rebels had taken control of parts of Ruhengeri, including a high-security prison where several major political prisoners were being held.[1]

We now know how significant the fight in Ruhengeri was on several fronts. For one, victory gave the RPF a strategic position in a regional stronghold of Hutu militancy. Second, it was proof positive of the RPF's comeback after three months spent training and regrouping in the Virunga Mountains, ending any speculation that it had merely faded away after its initial offensive narrowly failed. The RPF had taken up its mantle again to overthrow the government of President Juvénal Habyarimana and establish a Rwanda for all Rwandans, including the million refugees in exile beyond its border.

What had been a disorganized and disheartened group in October 1990 had become a well-organized and disciplined army under the direction of Major General Paul Kagame. "He organized us, told us the mission, the vision, and the objective, and then launched us afresh into the operational theater," recalled General James Kabarebe, who served as an aide de camp to Kagame in the RPF. As Kabarebe recalled, Kagame continuously preached to the troops that their mission was not limited to fighting and defending borders. Nor was security related to military action alone. "Your mission," Kagame told the RPF fighters from the beginning, "includes the social, political, and economic lives of the people of Rwanda."

Interestingly, the article stated that about 100 French paratroopers, based in Kigali, were sent to Ruhengeri, reportedly to evacuate French nationals and other foreigners. This was the third major significance of the battle: it gave Kagame and the RPF a taste of what was to come. In addition to their struggle against Rwandan armed forces, they would also face well-equipped and highly trained French fighters sent to support the Habyarimana regime.

The French were very visible allies to Rwanda under Habyarimana, providing financial and military aid. As Stephen Kinzer observed in A Thousand Hills, in the early 1990s France had sold the Rwandan government $20 million in weaponry and helped the country buy five times that amount from Egyptian and South African arms dealers, with purchases guaranteed by its government-owned Crédit Lyonnais bank.[2] Among the many theories about why France took such an interest in Rwanda was the apparent desire to keep the country part of *francophone* Africa rather than allow it to become part of the surrounding English-speaking region.

As the RPF won its first skirmishes against Rwandan forces, another battle was being waged in the country, this time of words. The extremist publication *Kangura* published the "Hutu Ten Commandments" in late 1990, spreading its gospel of hatred against the Tutsi. Under the commandments, a Hutu who married or befriended a Tutsi woman, or who engaged in a business partnership with a Tutsi, was considered a traitor. The commandments called for the Rwandan armed forces to be exclusively Hutu and declared, "Hutu should stop having mercy on the Tutsi." The ninth commandment called on Hutus to "have unity and solidarity and be concerned with the fate of their Hutu brothers," and to be "firm and vigilant against their common Tutsi enemy." The public campaign to promote Hutu Power, as the divisive ideology was called, was intensifying.[3]

By the end of 1991, the RPF and its fighters, known as the Rwandan Patriotic Army, controlled a large area along Rwanda's northern border, including the Mulindi tea plantation where Kagame established the headquarters for the RPF and from which he would direct the war for the next three years. As the RPF captured more ground, momentum changed. Although the RPF remained outnumbered and outgunned, the situation was far from dire. "We were on our own territory," recalled Rose

Kabuye, who had been a major in the RPF. "We saw that the political regime was weak. The 'Rwanda refugee boys' were winning."

For Habyarimana, the political landscape was also changing. He came under international pressure to legalize opposition parties, among them the Coalition pour la Défense de la République (CDR), an extremist group whose key organizers included the president's powerful and feared wife, Agathe Habyarimana. When the president announced his intention in 1991 to negotiate with the RPF to stop the costly civil war, extremists protested what they saw as his "middle of the road" appeasement. Soon, the CDR would unleash a demonic fury upon the country, polluting the airwaves with hateful propaganda, promoting genocide, and supporting the dreaded *interahamwe,* a paramilitary group trained to carry out terror and mass killings.

Extremist political factions such as the CDR were determined to derail the peace talks at all costs. A May 1992 *New York Times* news report described clashes among rival political parties in Kigali, in which several people were killed. The unrest, the report stated, came just before peace talks were to commence between the Habyarimana government and the RPF. Although Habyarimana's party blamed the RPF for a "surge in violence," which began in the countryside and later spread to the capital, opposition parties blamed "extreme right-wing elements" around President Habyarimana for "orchestrating violence as a way of discrediting democracy and clinging to power."[4]

Against this inflamed backdrop, peace talks between the Habyarimana regime and the RPF began in Arusha, Tanzania in July 1992. Kagame communicated every day with the RPF team. He was a natural negotiator with a seemingly intuitive sense of when to cede a point and when to remain steadfast. "They would tell him about snags in negotiations, and then he would give them advice: 'Please do this on this issue; be flexible but don't go beyond this,'" Kabarebe described.

As Kabarebe spoke with us, seated in an armchair in his office at the Ministry of Defense, a large framed photograph hung on the wall behind him. It showed several RPF fighters in military fatigues; for the Defense Minister, no doubt, it was a powerful and visible reminder of the struggle they all shared. In the center was Kagame, his rail-thin figure and eyeglasses unmistakable. What was striking about the picture was how young they all looked. When the photo was taken in 1992, Kagame was 35. At the time he took command of the RPF to lead the civil war for liberation and unification in October 1990, he had just turned 33. Yet already he was a battle-tested military strategist. And as the Arusha peace talks continued, Kagame would display other strengths—as a conciliator, diplomat, and tactician.

Protests against the peace process resulted in fresh waves of violence against Tutsis in which hundreds were killed as venomous rhetoric escalated. In November 1992, Léon Mugesera, a friend of Habyarimana and a colleague in his political party, gave a speech in which he incited party members to kill the Tutsi and dump their bodies into the rivers of Rwanda. According to Kinzer, "Speeches like this left no doubt what . . . Hutu radicals were plotting. They proposed, explicitly and quite seriously, to resolve Rwanda's conflict through a 'final solution' in which every Tutsi in the country—a total of more than one million people—would be killed or forced to flee."[5] (It was not until early 2012 that Mugesera, known as the "spokesman of hatred," was deported by Canada to stand trial in Rwanda for genocide crimes.)

In early 1993, gangs of killers raged through northern Rwanda, murdering more than 1,000 people. Outraged, Kagame announced that the RPF would pull out of the Arusha talks. In a show of might, he launched a new RPF offensive, with 8,000 fighters storming toward Kigali. Although they faced heavy resistance from Rwandan government troops backed by the French, the RPF pressed on. The international community, ignoring the escalating slaughter, recoiled at the RPF's apparent breach of the ceasefire and demanded the fighters abandon their new defensive positions outside the capital. To the shock of his soldiers, Kagame agreed to pull his troops back more than 90 kilometers, although he managed to gain a concession that established a demilitarized zone in the country as a condition for resuming the peace talks.

"It was very difficult to convince the fighters who had sacrificed a lot, to tell them to pick up their guns and go back," Kabarebe recalled. "But because of the respect he [Kagame] wielded, we believed that his decision was well thought out and well intentioned."

Kagame's words to the retreating fighters did not speak of defeat but of the confidence the RPF had gained with every kilometer as it had marched toward Kigali. "How did you reach here?" Kagame asked his troops.

"By fighting," they replied.

"Using what?" Kagame continued.

"Our guns."

"Did you capture even more?"

"Yes," the troops agreed.

"So what do you lose?" Kagame asked them. A skillful user of motivational rhetoric with a deep knowledge of human psychology, he helped the RPF savor a victory even as they returned to their previous zone of control far outside Kigali.

On August 4, 1993, all parties signed the Arusha peace accord, ending a three-year civil war. The RPF agreed to a ceasefire and declared its intention to transition from an army to a political party. But the integration of RPF troops into the Rwandan armed forces proved very difficult. At first, the Habyarimana regime would only concede a small percentage of the army to be made up by RPF; in the end, it was set at 40 percent, with the other 60 percent composed of troops loyal to the government. "It was a risk," Kabarebe admitted. "We feared that if we integrated they would finish us. They would kill us one by one and that would be the end of the RPF fighters."

In September 1993, the United Nations established the United Nations Assistance Mission to Rwanda (UNAMIR) and sent troops to the country as observers and peacekeepers. But as a 1999 report to the UN concluded, UNAMIR's mandate of neutrality without direct intervention—not even to stop the genocide—undermined its effectiveness. Its warnings went unheeded by the Security Council, and its presence in Rwanda was ultimately impotent.[6]

The signing of the peace accord, and efforts to establish a broad-based transitional government that included the RPF, did nothing to stop the hatred spewing regularly over the Rwandan airwaves. The infamous Radio Télévision Libre des Milles Collines (RTLMC), which was backed by the extremist CDR, stepped up its propaganda programming. In Rwandan culture, radio was an important means of communication and connection. RTLMC perverted that crucial channel with messages of violence and warnings that something big was coming. What that would be, no one knew for sure, but Rwanda was turning into a powder keg of anxiety and anticipation.

"Even months before the conclusion of the Arusha peace process, homes were already being marked," President Kagame told us, drawing an "X" in the air with his finger. "Everybody knew why they were doing it: they were marking homes of Tutsis. The [Habyarimana] government said it was for census. But they only marked homes of Tutsis, not everybody's home. And everybody knew about it. Not a single Western embassy didn't know about it."

The threat of genocide was also no secret to the United Nations. "Practice genocides" had occurred in the country for decades, starting with the violence of 1959 and continuing in the early 1960s during which Kagame was nearly killed. In January 1994, four months before the genocide began in earnest, the United Nations received sensitive information that indicated a murderous rampage was about to grip the country. An informant known as "Jean-Pierre" provided that information to UN forces in Rwanda, which were under the command of General Roméo Dallaire, a Canadian who commanded the UNAMIR international force of peacekeepers. Based on the informant's report, Dallaire cabled a military adviser to UN Secretary General Boutros Boutros-Ghali, reporting the existence of a plan to wipe out the Tutsi population. As Dallaire later told the UN in a report on the genocide, "It [the cable] should have been given the highest priority and attention and shared at the highest level." Instead, the opposite happened. The UN failed to act. Jean-Pierre disappeared.[7]

There were other visible signs of the plot in Rwanda, including huge quantities of machetes and weapons bought and stashed by militant forces behind the genocide. Warnings were whispered. "There are survivors who have said they had Hutu friends who used to tell them, 'Be careful. Why don't you find a place to go? Something is coming,'" Kagame related.

On April 6, 1994, President Habyarimana attended a regional meeting in Dar-es-Salaam, Tanzania, along with top leaders from Burundi, Kenya, and Tanzania, where they discussed the implementation of the Arusha agreement, which extremists still bitterly opposed. At the end of the meeting, Habyarimana boarded his presidential Falcon 50 jet, a present from French President Francois Mitterrand. President Cyprien Ntaryamira of Burundi asked if he could accompany Habyarimana. The plan was for the Rwandan president to get off in Kigali before the plane continued to Bujumbura, Burundi. Later that evening, as the jet approached Kigali airport, two missiles were fired into the night sky and hit the plane. It crashed into the garden of Habyarimana's house, where it burst into flames.

Who shot down the plane has remained a mystery, although many theories exist. One is that the extremist forces ordered the plane to be shot down. Another is that the RPF, on the order of Kagame himself, had shot down the plane, an allegation they have always strongly denied. In January 2012, a report from a French judge exonerated Kagame and the RPF leaders; based on where the missiles had been fired, it was not possible for the RPF to have launched them.

On the night of April 6, 1994, Kagame was watching the African cup soccer tournament on television—Senegal versus Cameroon—when he learned that Habyarimana's plane had crashed. First, he received a call from a commander who was leading a battalion stationed at the parliament building in Kigali, which had been sent there to protect RPF dignitaries working on the peace accord and the transitional government. "They heard something—an explosion. Then, 15 or 20 minutes later, some people rushed to the parliament building to take refuge," Kagame recalled. "They had been either near the place [of the plane crash] or they received phone calls that something had happened. They suspected it had something to do with the president."

Kabarebe brought him a note that confirmed those suspicions. When he learned that Habyarimana's plane had indeed crashed, Kagame tensed up as he contemplated what might happen next. Then, he ordered all troops to be put on "standby class 1"—a full alert.

The reaction was swift and violent. As the *interahamwe* paramilitary unleashed its fury, civilians joined the murderous spree. Neighbors killed neighbors; no place was safe. Within parliament, RPF dignitaries and others who had taken refuge in the building were holed up in the lower level, beyond the reach of mortar fire that left pockmarks, still visible today, on the outer walls. Among those inside the building was Rose Kabuye, who had been appointed by the RPF to serve in parliament. "We were there two weeks," Kabuye recalled. "The army did not get into the building. Our soldiers were in the trenches [surrounding parliament]. After about two weeks, they created a buffer zone." When Kabuye emerged, the scene shocked her: there were bodies everywhere.

Among the first victims of the genocide was Prime Minister Agathe Uwilingiyimana, a moderate Hutu, who had become the

constitutional head of government after Habyarimana's plane
was shot down. Knowing she and her family were in danger,
the prime minister fled to the nearby UN Development Program
compound. She was found there by the renegade Presidential
Guard, assaulted, and assassinated. The Presidential Guard also
had its murderous sights on another target: Ten Belgian paratroopers from UNAMIR who had been sent to guard the prime
minister. The Belgian soldiers were disarmed, arrested, and
taken to "Camp Kigali," the Rwandan armed forces compound.
As chaos and violence gripped Kigali, UNAMIR commander
Dallaire demanded to know their whereabouts. Finally, he was
told they could be found at Kigali hospital. In his memoir, *Shake
Hands with the Devil,* Dallaire related how he searched waiting
rooms and corridors, through a sea of blood and misery, until he
finally found the bodies. "At first I saw what seemed to be sacks
of potatoes to the right of the morgue door. It slowly resolved
in my vision into a heap of mangled and bloodied white flesh in
tattered Belgian para-command uniforms."[8]

After the killing of the soldiers, Belgium withdrew the rest
of its forces, further diminishing the UNAMIR presence. Despite
Dallaire's plea for more troops and the authority to use force to
stop the genocide, on April 22, 1994, the UN Security Council
voted unanimously to reduce the peacekeeping force in Rwanda
from 1,700 to about 270. The UN force was instructed to promote a ceasefire and assist with relief work, but not to intervene
to stop the violence.

As fighting escalated, diplomats, foreign aid workers, and
other foreign nationals were evacuated. Rwandans, however,
were not part of the rescue effort. People who attempted to rescue Rwandan friends were barred from doing so. Many never

even tried. Kagame shared a brief story of a relative who had worked for the UN in Kigali for many years. When the genocide began, other family members fled to her home until there were about nine of them altogether. As the militia attacked her home, she managed to call the UN before her phone line was cut, begging for help that never arrived. "They said they tried," Kagame said tersely, "but they never tried."

Inaction by the UN created a vacuum of leadership. Into that void stepped Kagame, who mobilized the RPF to do what the UN and the West refused to undertake. For the RPF, the mission was always unification of the country. As Kagame commented in a June 1994 interview with journalists who visited the RPF headquarters in Mulindi, "The first task is to make the Rwandans feel like they are Rwandans who have rights whether they are Hutu or Tutsi."[9] In the process, it would also have to stop one of the worst genocides in modern history.

In order to keep his focus, Kagame willed himself not to be overcome with anger by the egregious spectacles of horror the RPF encountered. As the Rwandan Patriotic Army advanced, troops encountered mass graves of people who had been hacked to death, women and children murdered, fetuses cut from the wombs of pregnant women. Sometimes, as bodies were turned over—a few of them still warm—survivors would be found, clinging to life. Three times Kagame was summoned by his commanders and aides to see what his soldiers had found: mass graves or the site of a brutal massacre. After the third episode, Kagame asked that he not be shown these horrors. "You would do me a good service if you did not bring that to my attention," Kagame told his staff. "Make sure I never see any of that again." The reason was simple, Kagame explained: each time he was a first-hand witness to the deaths and how brutally people were being killed, "everything about me changed. I got very angry." The leader of an army could not afford to lose his focus, particularly in the midst of a war with so many priorities.

According to the Convention for the Prevention and Punishment of the Crime of Genocide, adopted by the United Nations General Assembly in December 1948, genocide is intentional destruction of a national, ethnic, racial, or religious group, in whole or in part. The victims of genocides number in the tens or hundreds of thousands, possibly in the millions. Yet one cannot lose sight of the fact that mass killings are comprised of individual murders: men, women, and children. In Rwanda, the killings of a million people were carried out on a horrifically efficient scale: on average, 10,000 per day, 417 per hour, 7 per minute. Sometimes it was as easy for the *interahamwe* as setting up a roadblock. Those who tried to flee were stopped; the *interahamwe* demanded ID cards, and anyone who was a Tutsi was killed. Militants known to be HIV positive purposefully raped Tutsi women, infecting them and any resulting children, who would die slow deaths with little or no treatment. Militias hunted those in hiding; neighbors and friends turned informant to save themselves or because they succumbed to the hate propaganda that told them Tutsis were not human, that they were "cockroaches." Hutu who resisted were threatened with death, and those who hid Tutsis were often killed alongside them.

A PERSONAL STORY OF GENOCIDE

Beyond the numbers and statistics and the chilling memorials in Rwanda, there are the stories. These are the accounts of ordinary citizens, neither police nor military. They were targeted because of a word stamped on their identity cards: *Tutsi*.

Serge Rwigamba was 13 years old in April 1994 when dead bodies began appearing in the street and his family was threatened by squads of militia. Inexplicably, the militia did not make good on its threat at first; it initially only looted the family home, promising to return in a few days to finish them off. Serge and his family left their home and stayed with their neighbors, and then the following evening joined others who were seeking refuge in a Catholic chapel nearby. In past killing sprees, church property had meant sanctuary; this time it was different.

Among the 300 or so people gathered in the chapel, it was decided that, in case of attack by the militia, everyone would be required to fight regardless of age, including women and children. Men were stationed at the front of their defenses to confront anyone who tried to enter the chapel grounds. Early one morning, when Serge was outside the chapel near the fence surrounding the property, he saw a large crowd approaching. Among the militia were the familiar faces of neighbors. The man in charge of the group, who wore a big hat and carried a gun and axes, had been a close friend of his father's; now he was leading a group armed with machetes on a silent march to the chapel.

Realizing the danger, Serge ran and told others what he had seen. They tried to resist, but were soon overpowered by the militia without a fight. A militia leader ordered women and children to be moved from the chapel to the main church nearby. The men who were left at the chapel, including Serge's father and half brother, were killed.

As Serge walked toward the church, he thought of the priest whom he had served as an acolyte at mass and who had always been friendly with his parishioners. He expected the priest to greet them warmly, to take them into the church and make sure they were safe. This time, he met them with a scornful laugh, accusing them and the other Tutsis of killing President Habyarimana. Confused, Serge had no idea what the priest was saying; his mother and father had killed no one.

Inside the church compound, Serge saw countless others who had fled their homes, looking for safety. Over the next month, many more would join them, including families of the militia who sought refuge in the church, believing that when RPF troops reached the capital, it would mean death to Hutus. For those who were Tutsi, the church was a prison camp; deaths from starvation and disease became more common. For the Hutu, access to the outside world was still permissible.

As for the priest, not only did he fail to protect them; he allowed the military to come into the church to carry out killings. Rather than shooting randomly, the killers were discriminating to be sure they were targeting Tutsis. By mid-June, as the RPF neared the city, the killers stepped up their efforts to kill as many of those at the church as possible. People were made to stand in groups as the killers pointed out their next intended victims. As Serge stood there, they picked people behind him and beside him, and two close friends who had stood right in front of him. The agony of waiting and wondering when he would be picked became torture; being selected began to seem a blessing. Considering himself already dead, Serge preoccupied himself with thoughts of heaven.

Toward the end, in one six-hour period, 157 people at the church were killed. Then, it stopped. The killers left, but said they would be back. As the survivors waited, terrified, they could not bring themselves to leave the church because they believed it meant certain death. Finally, on the night of July 3,

1994, the atmosphere began to change. A former lieutenant in the Rwandan army told them the RPF was nearby. Rescue had come. Serge finally began to believe he might live.

Today, Serge is a guide officer at the Kigali Memorial Centre, where the bodies of his father and half brother are buried. As he stoically told his story, Serge pondered his personal legacy as a genocide survivor, and what that horrific episode will mean to those who will come after him. "The children I will have one day will live with the scars of the past," he said, "but they will look at it as history."

In his award-winning book, *We Wish to Inform You That Tomorrow We Will be Killed with Our Families,* author Philip Gourevitch collected stories about the genocide from those who survived to tell of the most efficient mass killing since the atomic bombings of Hiroshima and Nagasaki. After three years of "looking around Rwanda and listening to Rwandans," the author found the horror of it—"the idiocy, the waste, and the sheer wrongness"—to be "uncircumscribable." In his book, Gourevitch quotes a priest, Abbé Modeste, in Butare, Rwanda's second-largest city, who observed, "Every survivor wonders why he is alive." The obvious answer, Gourevitch noted, is that the RPF had come to the rescue. But in the case of Abbé Modeste, the RPF did not reach Butare in the south until mid-July, and roughly 75 percent of the Tutsis in Rwanda had been killed by early May. "In this regard, at least, the genocide had been entirely successful; to those who were targeted, it was not death but life that seemed an accident of fate."[10]

There is a thread of destiny in some of the stories Kagame shared with us, of narrow escapes and near misses. Although he declined to interpret the circumstances as providential, it's tempting to think it. But as Kagame explained with a smile, "I deal with life here on earth, with what I know and what I see. It is a pastor's job to deal with life somewhere else." Yet he also admitted that, as he looks back on the war, he is surprised he was successful in what he had to accomplish as commander in charge. Any number of circumstances—for example, when a mortar killed two nearby people but he was left standing—could have had other outcomes. "Sometimes you can see that the way things work out is not because of you. Brothers who have done the same things or who were in a similar situation failed, but you do not," he added.

Kagame told a story of walking with the troops for several hours and then stopping to rest. As he looked for a place to sit down, he noticed a section of the roadway that was raised, providing a kind of seat. From the look of the ground, others had used this spot for the same purpose. He lowered himself slowly and loosened the laces of his boots. Relaxing, he leaned forward, elbows resting against his thighs. When he got up, he stood without boosting himself. Only then did he discover he had been sitting on a booby trap: a huge bomb wired with grenades and landmines, enough explosives to level a building.

"If I had put my hands like this"—Kagame pantomimed placing his hands palms-down beside him—"or if I had leaned back on my elbows to rest," the bomb would have detonated. "That incident is not something I could take credit for," Kagame said. "I had actually screwed up. If you sit where others have sat, it could be a trap."

Reflecting on other events, Kagame said there were many incidents during the war that could have turned out differently; for example, if troops had failed to carry out orders or, conversely, if they failed to adjust their actions based on changing conditions. "Overall, despite the magnitude of problems and the few resources we had, we managed to get through. You have to start wondering: how did it happen?" Kagame said.

How did a group of refugees, many of whom had never been to Rwanda before, become a highly effective and committed fighting force that liberated the country to claim the birthright for all Rwandans? How did they stand up to an enemy backed by a European superpower and show the world they were more than a "band of rebels"? One answer is that the RPF was more disciplined and better organized than the Rwandan army forces. The fighters were able to overcome the odds because of the strength of their convictions that the war was for unity and a future for all Rwandans. As Kagame told journalists in June 1994, "We have been refugees for more than three decades. This is the first time I'm traveling through the country. I feel I'm part of the country. I've never felt that feeling before. Wherever I was, I was a refugee. It's certainly a very good experience to feel you have an identity."[11]

On July 4, 1994, the RPF reached its goal and captured Kigali. Two weeks later, a transitional government was in place. Although the genocide had finally ended, Rwanda was still dangerous, with insurgency and threats against the newly established order. During and after the war, a French buffer area within the country, known as the Turquoise Zone, had become a haven for former *genocidaires*. From the protection of the zone, these perpetrators fled to Zaire, which is now known as the Democratic Republic of the Congo (DRC), after the conflict.

The devastation of the country was so great, and the legacy of the genocide so traumatic, that the country was "widely considered as an irremediably failed state," the Rwandan government stated in a background paper on state-building for a conference held in November 2011 in Kigali. A staggering number of people were dead, and hundreds of thousands were directly culpable. "This created a profoundly shattered social fabric: 75 percent of the Tutsi population inside the country had been killed, as well as the vast majority of the moderate political and civic voices. Although the genocide had been brought to an end, the bulk of the army, militia, and political class who had carried it out crossed over to the neighboring Democratic Republic of the Congo determined to resume the genocidal fight," the paper stated.[12]

From havens in eastern Congo, the former *genocidaires* continued to wage assaults on Rwanda until controversial strikes by Rwandan troops, which resulted in a UN investigation into alleged atrocities committed in the Congo, diminished that threat. While the war was over and the genocide had finally ended, peace and stability were not established in Rwanda until about 2000. These factors add to the political and diplomatic complexity facing Rwanda even today, as it deals with threats from former *genocidaires* as well as criticism from outsiders on the way it enforces security.

Immediately after the war, however, the new political leadership needed to deal with the crushing aftermath. A million people had been killed. Two million lived outside the borders of the country. As some refugees returned, others fled in fear of what might come next. Yet Rwanda, though deeply damaged, was not dead. It could be reborn as a new nation, building on the common ground of one people, one language, one culture to overcome the bitter enmity that lingered. To do so, it needed to embrace reconciliation and unification the way no other group or country had before, and turn these ideals into daily reality for Rwandans everywhere. This would require extraordinary sacrifice and courage, and profound leadership that could not fail.

4

RECONCILIATION
AND UNIFICATION

Bishop John Rucyahana stretched out his arm and held a water glass about three feet off the ground. "If I drop it from this level, it will certainly break, but in fewer and larger pieces than if it drops from a higher level." To illustrate the point, he raised his arm above his head. "The higher up you go with the glass, the more pieces there will be." Setting the glass back on the table, the Anglican bishop, one of Rwanda's most influential spiritual leaders and the head of the country's National Unity and Reconciliation Commission, continued his parable. "Rwanda was crushed from a higher level into so many pieces."

Rucyahana witnessed the devastation firsthand. Immediately after the genocide, Rucyahana, who was born in Rwanda but lived much of his life in Uganda, led a team of clergy to view the aftermath of the brutality and to minister to the people. What they found shocked and horrified them: dead bodies and decomposing corpses, mass graves, traumatized survivors, and thousands of orphans. "We needed to see the horrors, as fresh as they were. I didn't want anyone to interpret it for us," he said. Of the ten pastors who went, four were badly traumatized; one had to be hospitalized. "The purpose was not to get ourselves sick," Rucyahana added. "If we were to be useful to this society, to counsel the people, we needed to understand the heinous acts and experiences that people had gone through."

What Rucyahana found was a nation in ruins, for which the church was as guilty as any other institution: from the Catholic Church's role in creating ethnic tensions under colonialism to the complicity of some (but certainly not all) pastors in killings that occurred during the genocide. "Your conscience as a human being demands that you take responsibility," he continued. "We failed the gospel. But, should we surrender and fail forever? Or, should we now do better?"

This rhetorical question goes to the heart of the country's commitment to reconciliation, forgiveness, and unification—its determination to overcome the sins of the past and stake a claim to a new and hopeful future. Restoring Rwanda for all Rwandans and providing a homeland to which refugees could return—the key goals of the Rwandan Patriotic Front (RPF)—became principles of national leadership and governance postgenocide. "We knew from the start that the process was reconciliation and integration," President Paul Kagame told us. "We wanted to address the problems that Rwanda had in the past, which were the result of bad politics. That's why our country became what it was. We believed that with different leadership and politics, the country would be different."

For unification to happen, reconciliation had to come first. A nation divided by terror and hatred had to find a way to live together as one. Although church leaders such as Rucyahana are involved in the reconciliation initiative, it is not based on any religion or denomination. Rather, it is a national policy, congruent with Rwanda's cultural values, which promote a sense of community. The policy is backed by leaders at the highest level, including the president and parliament.

Today, all the moving parts that go into that reconciliation are interconnected, raising the stakes for its success. To be effective, it must permeate every part of the country, from the prison ministry and the military to local villages where survivors and perpetrators live next door to each other. In schools, where students previously had to identify themselves as Hutu or Tutsi and discrimination was commonplace, the new lesson is common ancestry, one language, and one culture.

Since the genocide, reconciliation has become the key underpinning of virtually every initiative in Rwanda, as laid out in its Vision 2020 plan: compulsory education, universal health care, and plans to develop a knowledge-based economy to improve the country's standard of living. At the same time, reconciliation depends upon education, health care, and poverty reduction to be effective. People must have confidence in the government, in each other, and in themselves before they can buy into a sweeping vision of reform and progress and see their places within it.

"Our unity, therefore, becomes our strength, our power," Rucyahana observed. "We cannot have sustainable strategic development when we are dismantled ourselves. You cannot have Vision 2020 when you are not united. We need people who think together, who think alike, who love each other, who trust each other, and own what we do together."

Rucyahana believes strongly that reconciliation is not a solution that can be imported from elsewhere. Only Rwanda can heal its own wounds, with a process that reflects its own cultural values. By the same token, reconciliation cannot be mandated, only facilitated. Indeed, even among the people we spoke to, attitudes toward reconciliation ranged from wholehearted embrace to those who understood the concept but still struggled to forgive the murderers of relatives and friends. Like much of the change in Rwanda (and elsewhere), it is also generational: it is more difficult for older people to change their viewpoints. After being told for most of their lives about distinct and opposing groups, they now find it hard to trust that Rwanda is one nation of one people. Younger people, unsurprisingly, more readily buy into Rwanda's postgenocide image of itself as a country of opportunity, in which education, development, and entrepreneurship are emphasized.

Admittedly, Rwanda is a country in transition—politically, economically, and socially. In order to appreciate just how far it has come, one must consider the starting point in July 1994, a time of complete chaos, devastation, and breakdown in civil order.

As Rwandan Foreign Minister Louise Mushikiwabo recalled the challenges immediately after the genocide, she closed her eyes for a moment as if to envision the scene. "Think back to the summer of 1994 and try to picture what was going on here, with three million Rwandans living outside the country and one million people dead. Infrastructure was destroyed. The whole fabric of our 'Rwandan-ness' no longer existed. Our country faced a humongous task of just living and getting back to the normal business of life."

Electricity, food, drinking water, and order and security were the priorities. Angry survivors with guns wanted to retaliate, which presented a security challenge for the RPF. A logistical nightmare ensued when refugees from the pogroms of the 1960s flooded back into the country to find what had been their property was occupied by others. To settle disputes, property was often divided or alternative tracts of government-owned land parceled out. Even the Akagera National Park had to be reduced by more than half in order to provide parcels of land for returning refugees. The government tried to be fair to all parties, but compromises often left one or both unsatisfied, particularly since Rwanda is a tiny country with scarce available land.

Housing remained a major challenge for the first several years, recalled Rose Kabuye, who served as mayor of Kigali from 1994 to 1998. She told us of one family that fled after the war ended, leaving an empty house that was then occupied by refugees returning from East Africa. When the original family returned a year or two later and discovered other people living in the house, the government had to step in to mediate. "I had to say, 'The owner of the house is here; you have to leave.' That was a big problem," Kabuye recalled. "It took so many years, so many disputes. That was a big challenge."

Another significant challenge postgenocide was establishing a transitional government that would include not only RPF leaders, but also Rwandans who had been part of previous regimes but who now supported the RPF. Kagame faced tremendous pressure to seek the presidency, but he declined and advocated for another appointee: a Hutu who had joined the RPF from the previous government regime. After nearly six years in office, the president of the transitional government, Pasteur Bizimungu, was removed from his position on charges of corruption. (He was subsequently convicted and imprisoned.) Kagame then became president of the transitional government in 2000; he was elected to serve a seven-year term in the country's first democratic election in 2003 and reelected in 2010 for a second seven-year term.

Looking back, Kagame said he had never wanted to become president immediately after the genocide, nor did that factor into his motivation for participating in the struggle to unify Rwanda. He defends the choice of someone who grew up inside the country as the first president postgenocide, as opposed to a Rwandan refugee like himself. He acknowledges how hard some people pushed for him to lead the transitional government, but in the end, he stuck to his conviction and became vice president and minister of defense, roles in which "I had to deal with more than enough problems."

Although the genocide ended when the RPF reached Kigali, security remained a major concern. The dreaded *interahamwe* militia drove masses of frightened Rwandans out of the country with propaganda about retaliatory killings, stoking fears that an RPF victory meant revenge on everyone else. As the people streamed toward the border to Zaire (now the Democratic Republic of the Congo), the *interahamwe* infiltrated the group, thus escaping Rwanda undetected into the protection of humanitarian aid camps. Suddenly the world, which had turned its back on the genocide, leaped to help the new Rwandan refugees, who unbeknownst to them included many of the *genocidaires* who had masterminded and committed mass killings.

In her firsthand account of the genocide and aftermath, author Immaculée Ilibagiza described how tens of thousands of the *interahamwe* sowed mass hysteria among ordinary people who abandoned their villages and fled to the refugee camps, where many died of disease and starvation. From within Zaire, the *interahamwe* then attempted to destabilize the Rwandan government. Ilibagiza described how, after the genocide, her home village near the border of Zaire was threatened nightly by killers who crossed the border back into Rwanda to take revenge on survivors. "Zaire had become infected with the cruel, homicidal hatred so deeply rooted in the hearts of Rwanda's extremist killers, and the disease began to spread," Ilibagiza wrote.[1]

Adding to the fear, the genocide sparked some retaliatory killings by soldiers immediately afterward. In our conversation, President Kagame spoke of some Rwandan Patriotic Army (RPA) soldiers who, in violation of orders, killed those whom they thought were responsible for the deaths of genocide victims. Kagame recalled the case of a soldier who killed the alleged perpetrators he believed had murdered his family and then committed suicide. The soldier left a note: he felt he had nothing to live for and knew he would be punished for his actions, so he killed himself. Although it gives few details of specific cases or numbers of people allegedly killed by soldiers in retaliation, the Kagame administration is adamant that the guilty soldiers were arrested by military police, tried, and punished. These incidents, Kagame explained to us, illustrate the "broader complexity of what we had to deal with" immediately after the genocide.

Another of Rwanda's pressing domestic problems postgenocide was its prison population, numbering more than 120,000 in a country with a population of less than six million at the time.

Although Rwanda remained committed to reconciliation and unification, there also needed to be a sense of justice so people knew perpetrators were being held accountable. The United Nations Security Council created the International Criminal Tribunal for Rwanda in Arusha, Tanzania, to prosecute those who were responsible for genocide and "serious violations of international humanitarian law" committed in Rwanda during calendar year 1994. The international tribunal set a precedent that finally gave the heinous crimes the name of *genocide*. For those who would later try to rewrite history or deny the genocide, the existence of the international tribunal and its proceedings provide irrefutable evidence.

The international tribunal lists among its achievements the arrest and prosecution of more than 70 people accused of involvement, including former Prime Minister Jean Kambanda (who was convicted and sentenced to life imprisonment) and several other members of the former government, as well as senior military leaders and high-ranking officials. The tribunal website lists nine other people who are accused and at large.

Below the high-visibility cases of masterminds who carried out the deaths of thousands of people, there was an exhaustive number of lower-level cases of alleged perpetrators who were being held in Rwandan prisons. Given the state of the Rwandan judicial system after the genocide, it was estimated it would take more than 200 years to try all cases. Indeed, by 1999, five years after the genocide, only 6,000 of 120,000 detainees had been tried.

To help adjudicate these cases, Rwanda turned to a traditional justice system known as *gacaca,* which means "patch of grass." *Gacaca* is part of Rwanda's cultural heritage and had been used in the past to settle disputes between neighbors or over property, but never at the level of genocide crimes and not at the number and scope of pending cases. *Gacaca* law established three levels, or categories, of crimes. Category 1 included planners of the genocide and people who held positions of authority; these cases were handled by the international tribunal and the Rwandan national courts. Category 2 crimes were murder and bodily harm, while Category 3 was solely property crime. *Gacaca* courts at the local or "cell" level, which includes several neighborhoods or small villages, heard Category 3 cases. At the next level up, known as the sector, which includes several cells, Category 2 cases were heard. In the *gacaca* process, defendants were encouraged to confess in exchange for a reduced sentence, while victims were encouraged to forgive. Human rights observers have voiced concerns over *gacaca* proceedings, particularly around the rights of the accused to be defended, but Rwanda remains committed to the process, citing its effectiveness and efficiency, particularly given the dearth of alternatives.

"What were we going to do in this country where all the lawyers were gone? If not dead, they had run away from the country. With no lawyers, how do you process 120,000 cases? Do you hold people in jail with no files?" Rucyahana asked. "The best way was our cultural way of solving and resolving disputes and judging cases."

Foreign Minister Mushikiwabo shook her head at the accusations that *gacaca* was imperfect, that not every trial was fair, and that grudges and jealousies could make the process far from impartial. "They are talking about fairness?" she retorted. "We are talking about common sense. Whatever you do in terms of justice is going to be imperfect, but it's a measure of how much good can you get out of a bad situation." Dealing with the aftermath of genocide in a country that lacked legal and financial resources was nearly impossible. Mushikiwabo continued, "So we asked ourselves, is there anything in our practices that can help us achieve a level of justice, that will allow us to gather the truth, try to reconcile, and, at the same time, achieve classic justice? Say '*gacaca*,' and every Rwandan understands."

Even the international tribunal acknowledged the effectiveness of the *gacaca* system. Judge Erik Møse, president of the tribunal, noted in October 2003 that "the ordinary Rwanda courts have been supplemented by the establishment of so-called *gacaca* courts, based on traditional justice, including lay judges, confessions and reconciliations." All levels of justice, he added, were not mutually exclusive, "but supplement each other and can all contribute to justice and reconciliation in Rwanda."[2]

From justice came another mission: the reintegration of prisoners into communities, with the perpetrator and the family of the victim living side by side. "It's of no use to have everybody condemned and not helped to recover from guilt," said Rucyahana. As a minister he practices what he preaches; in a PBS interview, he stated that he forgave those who had killed his niece, who "peeled off the flesh of her arms to the wrist, and they left bare bones, and they gang-raped her." He forgave them, he explained, "because forgiving is not only benefiting the criminal, it benefits me."[3]

Rucyahana told us of one man he counseled in his prison ministry who had killed 40 people, after which he lost all sense of being human. For perpetrators like him, death would have been preferable; asking pardon and forgiveness seemed impossible. "We are all those broken pieces: those who are sick from the guilt, from the hurt and despair, and from the anger, pain, and loss," he added. "When you put them on a scale, the guilt on one side and the loss and anger on the other, they will balance. Out of that, you have to make a nation."

In the eyes of the Rwandan government, *gacaca* facilitated the prosecution of the majority of those involved in the genocide while putting an end to a cycle of impunity. Judgments ranged from five to ten years to life sentences (5 to 8 percent of verdicts), while acquittals made up 20 to 30 percent of the verdicts. Testimony from *gacaca* proceedings has helped survivors find the remains of loved ones and provide a decent burial. Equally important, *gacaca* paved the way for repentant convicts to return to communities under conditions that, while imperfect, were acceptable to both victims and perpetrators.

Reconciliation and forgiveness on a national level require involvement from every facet of society. One of the most interesting initiatives has involved the RPF and the RPA, which integrated soldiers from the Forces Armées Rwandaises (FAR), the former national army. FAR soldiers who were captured and willing to adopt RPF ideology were welcomed into the ranks of the liberating army. Convincing government forces to fight alongside RPF troops was also essential to gaining political support, President Kagame told us. He cited the Ugandan struggle, where rebels led by Yoweri Museveni were a tiny force with huge political support. In contrast, RPF grew larger than the Ugandan resistance but lacked the political support. "So we had to . . . grow the political support. This was a hard task," Kagame explained. "We had to combine a just cause and a military force to turn things around and [win] political support in our favor."

The RPF's approach stands in stark contrast to the former FAR, which excluded Tutsis from serving. Defense Minister

James Kabarebe told us that from 1960 to 1990, only one Tutsi
served in the Rwandan army. The RPF, which had been composed originally of refugees from Tutsi backgrounds, could not
risk falling into the same trap as the FAR by being exclusionary.
"In Africa, people look at the military in a different way: he
who has the gun has authority over you," Kabarebe explained.
"Here, people saw their sons in the countryside, and they saw
Hutu and Tutsi soldiers together and serving the same purpose.
Reconciliation started with the military."

Rwanda's formal military demobilization and integration
had two phases. Between September 1997 and February 2001,
18,692 RPA soldiers were demobilized, while 15,000 ex-FAR
soldiers were integrated into the RPA. In the second phase, 2001
to 2008, military forces were reduced and 40,000 soldiers and
ex-combatants were demobilized. "The gradual integration of
ex-FAR into the RPA early in the aftermath of the genocide was
considered the military parallel of the formation of the Government of National Unity," the Rwandan government stated in
a report on nation building. "Rather than simply demobilizing
former combatants, the programme was conceived as a peace-
building mechanism in its own right."[4]

Nationally, the process of reconciliation and unification
seeks to end the divide of Hutu and Tutsi. "We have created
one tribe, which is being Rwandan. We have created an environment that has turned Rwanda into a country with opportunities," Kagame added. However, like much about postgenocide
Rwanda, there are no easy answers or convenient solutions that
please everyone. On the one hand, a national policy strongly encourages forgiveness and reconciliation; on the other, there is the

need to honor victims and survivors of genocide. Some argue, understandably, that people have a right to their victimhood.

"It is an incredibly difficult balance, allowing survivors to express what they experienced without being forced into reconciliation and forgiveness," commented Karen Jungblut, director of research and documentation for the Shoah Foundation, which was created by movie director Steven Spielberg to gather and preserve oral histories from Holocaust survivors, and later expanded to include the Rwandan genocide. During a recent visit to Shoah, visitors from the Kigali Memorial Centre, who are themselves survivors of the Rwandan genocide, were learning best practices for gathering and archiving oral histories so they will be preserved in perpetuity and made available to scholars. Giving "a voice to the voiceless" through oral histories helps survivors retain pieces of their lives and furthers efforts to raise awareness in the global community, which may prevent such horrors from being repeated elsewhere.

Jungblut acknowledged that Rwandan leadership, and Kagame in particular, is faced with the incredible challenge of "doing it all at the same time," from memorializing the past to promoting reconciliation and advancing the country's economic development. "He has that full spectrum of responsibilities," she added. "Anyone would be stopped in their tracks by it."

Unifying Rwanda also includes outreach to another important population: refugees who remain in other countries, including Uganda, Burundi, and the Democratic Republic of the Congo. Among them are people who left decades ago, as well as those who fled following the genocide because they feared retaliation.

Although Rwanda is the most densely populated country in Africa (10.7 million people in 10,000 square miles), it continues to welcome its refugees home. "Even though Rwanda is small geographically, it doesn't mean we don't need our people. The greatest resource we have is our people," Rucyahana said. "Their increase is not detrimental to us."

The Foreign Ministry has been involved in outreach to the Rwandan diaspora, helping to disseminate a message of welcome. The Department of Diaspora organizes "come and see" trips back to Rwanda for people who are curious about their homeland, including those who have never been to the country but for whom Rwanda holds a powerful emotional tie. "One thing that is very heartening is the young people who want to come here. Maybe they saw the president on CNN or they are talking to Rwandan friends on Facebook—we have a lot of that. They come to visit, and then they want to come back and settle," Foreign Minister Mushikiwabo explained.

According to government figures, of 3.5 million refugees recorded in July 1994, only 70,000 remained outside the country as of late 2011. In addition to Rwandans who fled, there are many people who call the country home even though they had never been there. Many grew up in other parts of Africa, Europe, or the United States, became educated, and started careers and even families there. Even though they put down roots elsewhere, Rwanda never stopped calling to them.

Jackie Karuletwa-Kakiza was born of Rwandan parents and spent many of her early years in Kenya; later she was educated at UCLA. She and her husband, Colin Muhoozi Kakiza, who is Ugandan and also graduated from UCLA after attending Westmont College in Santa Barbara, spent several more years in the

United States, including as employees of Four Seasons Hotels and Resorts. After an impromptu meeting with Kagame in Los Angeles, the couple decided to move to Rwanda in early 2010 with their daughter, Shema, who was then turning five. Amazingly, Karuletwa-Kakiza had never even visited Rwanda before moving there. For her, it had only existed in her parents' memories and stories.

Today, the Kakizas are consultants in the hospitality industry, recruiting and training employees in Western standards of customer service. When we met them, they were working with the biggest hotels in Kigali, including the Serena, in the heart of Kigali; the famed Hotel des Milles Collines, better known as "Hotel Rwanda," from the movie by the same name; and other organizations. Their consulting firm, Kazibora, has recently begun working in the banking sector, as well. As Rwanda continues to develop, the couple sees an opportunity to advance, as well as an obligation to give back.

The Rwandan diaspora also includes older people who may fear that, because of their actions or their support of the former regime, they could face accusations upon returning. For Bishop Rucyahana, the message of reconciliation and forgiveness is as important for them as it is for those at home. "We don't want our people to remain undercover because of the association of guilt . . . because they carry the guilt of their fathers," he added. "We want them to be competent wherever they are. If they want to come home, let them come."

Of course, healing must start on the individual level. It is one thing to talk about forgiveness and unity, and it is another for people living side by side to trust each other. The country's National Unity and Reconciliation Commission (NURC) measures its progress on achieving reconciliation, surveying people aged 18 and older. More than 90 percent are rural residents. The NURC rates national harmony on the basis of several variables, including political culture, human security, citizenship and identity, transitional justice, understanding the past, and social cohesion. An October 2010 report known as the *Rwanda Reconciliation Barometer* showed that in every category, the majority of those surveyed felt progress has been made. For example, the survey indicated more than 97 percent of Rwandans feel proud of being citizens of the country and want their children to think of themselves as Rwandan as opposed to being Hutu, Tutsi, or Twa.

The report, however, also indicated Rwanda still had progress to make, especially in areas such as access to land and housing and compensation to genocide survivors. Interestingly, the report concluded that it is not ethnicity but rather "economic cleavages" that divide Rwandan society today.[5] This increases the pressure on the development initiatives to improve prosperity and provide opportunity for all, particularly those at the bottom of the socioeconomic pyramid. Over and again we encountered this theme: self-determination on the national level had to be mirrored, embraced, and experienced on the local level. The government cannot carry out these efforts alone. Private enterprise and foreign investment are critical to providing opportunity, particularly as the younger generation is educated. Even on the local level, reconciliation can foster productivity in basic agriculture and the raising of cows and goats. Instead of staking animals on a farmer's tiny plot of land, combining land owned by several farmers (who may have come from different ethnic groups) makes for better grazing.

Among the many examples of reconciliation, opportunity, and economic development we came across, one of the most inspiring was the story told by Joy Ndungutse, founder of Gahaya Links, a for-profit Rwandan handicraft company. Today, its products, including baskets and jewelry with traditional and authentic Rwandan designs, are sold in the United States by retailers, including Macy's and Anthropologie. But it started with one Rwandan woman with a car, who left her home in Uganda and followed her heart back to Rwanda with her children immediately after the genocide. Despite the complete devastation she found, Ndungutse remained committed to finding a way to help women traumatized by what they had endured. She approached the transitional government established by the RPF, but there were no money or resources available. Many of the officials she met with worked out of offices that were little more than shells; some had no tables or chairs. If she wanted to help, Ndungutse was told, she was more than welcome, but she'd have to do it on her own.

Unsure of where to start, Ndungutse found a woman working with her husband in a field. Ndungutse called her aside and told the woman she wanted to help. If the woman would bring friends, Ndungutse would meet them the next day. When she returned, 20 women were sitting under a tree waiting. "I am not a donor," Ndungutse explained. "I have no money, but I have skills for what we used to do when we were young. This was weaving. I am going to train you."

Over time, more women came for classes on weaving, until the group grew too large for Ndungutse to handle by herself. She persuaded her sister, Janet, to join her in a mission to empower women. In time, Ndungutse, who had lived in the United States for 15 years, connected with a New York–based importer. The response from the American market was good; a red basket marketed for Valentine's Day produced an order for 1,000, which had to be made in two months. With that order and a flurry of production, Gahaya Links was launched.

Beyond the production and marketing of products to help women support themselves and their families, the cooperatives became a catalyst for forgiveness and reconciliation on the individual level. As the women came together, old conflicts, resentments, and deep hurt were harbored by many, who included victims and relatives of perpetrators. Ndungutse realized that without healing, the cooperatives could not continue. She gathered the women together, just as she had in the early days of training, this time with a different message. "There is no way you can make a beautiful basket if your heart is not clean. You say there is no way you can forgive this woman whose husband murdered your children. But you have to come to believe so you can erase your anger. We cannot do much without reconciliation. It must take place."

The women sat in silence, their eyes focused on their weaving. Finally, a woman stood up. "I have something to say," she began and turned to another woman in the room. "Today I forgive you. Your husband killed my children, but you did not." With hugs and tears, the women cried and prayed, and then went back to weaving. Over and over, the scene was repeated in a catharsis of confession and forgiveness as the women worked together.

Reconciliation and forgiveness are not simply ideals, but a strategy being carried out on the national, regional, local, and individual levels. The country continues to make strides to unify as it moves beyond the scourge of genocide and leverages its cultural values and traditions to help Rwanda strive for and realize goals of collective well-being, prosperity, and economic development for all. Rwanda knows the stakes are high.

5

RWANDA'S CEO

In the late 1990s, the Monitor Group, a Boston-based consulting firm, was under contract with the World Bank to work with several developing countries, including Zambia, Mozambique, Bangladesh, Nigeria, and Romania. The purpose was to help these countries improve their competitive positions and increase their exports while, at the same time, establishing better relationships with the World Bank. The modus operandi for developing countries in those days—and it's largely unchanged today—was to conform with whatever the World Bank deemed best, from trade practices to currency valuation, as a prerequisite for receiving aid. The World Bank approached the Monitor Group in 1999 to work with Rwanda, acting as outside facilitators at a government retreat to formulate a long-term vision. By the time the retreat was scheduled in 2000, Rwanda had a new president: Paul Kagame.

Kaia Miller was the first consultant from the Monitor Group to meet Kagame in person. Miller, who today runs Aslan Global, a Boston-based consulting firm that advises entrepreneurs and government leaders in emerging markets, recalled for us her impressions of the new Rwandan president: young (he was 42 at the time), smart, unassuming, highly approachable, and open to new ideas. In their first face-to-face meeting, they discussed the retreat, which was a forum for Rwanda to identify its priorities and set forth strategies for achieving its vision. Then she put it in different terms. "The whole purpose," Miller told Kagame, "is to get Rwanda in a position to say 'No, thank you' to the World Bank."

With that, Kagame extended his hand and told her, "That's exactly what I'm trying to do."

On a continent in which foreign aid is often the main source—and sometimes the only source—of funds, Kagame has led Rwanda on a radically different path: toward self-determination and self-sufficiency. As Kagame later reflected in his essay "The Backbone of a New Rwanda," published in the book *In the River They Swim: Essays from Around the World on Enterprise Solutions to Poverty*: "Many leaders are overly influenced by the multilateral institutions and by bilateral donors. We have had the strange benefit that, early on, not a lot of nations wanted to give us foreign aid, and we turned that into an advantage."[1]

Instead of pandering for foreign aid, Rwanda differentiated itself by fostering economic development. From his earliest days as president, when Rwanda was mired in endemic poverty and still needed to develop basic infrastructure, Kagame was already thinking about wealth creation and the importance of the private sector as the means to elevate the country.

By the time he met Kagame, Michael Fairbanks of the Monitor Group had worked with five presidents of Colombia, two prime ministers of Bermuda, Peruvian President Alberto

Fujimori, and Fidel Castro of Cuba, among others. For him, Kagame stood out early on as a new kind of leader and a bit of a paradox. Here was a former African general who believed in entrepreneurship. As the new president, Kagame was not interested in marketing himself or ingratiating himself with the international community; instead, he emphasized doing the right thing and letting the results speak for themselves.

At the retreat, Fairbanks and Miller saw another side of Kagame's leadership: his willingness to immerse himself in the details. During the sessions, they discussed several topics crucial to Rwanda's postgenocide transformation, including building innovation and competitiveness, economic reforms, developing an information and communication technology (ICT) strategy, and defining Rwanda's national imperatives. What greatly impressed the Monitor Group facilitators was Kagame's active participation all five days, including one of the breakout sessions on developing tourism. Even when he excused himself to use the restroom, Kagame asked that the facilitators wait until he returned before continuing the discussion; he didn't want to miss anything. "What president does that?"commented Fairbanks, who today is cofounder of the SEVEN fund, a philanthropic foundation that produces films, books, and research to foster enterprise solutions to global poverty, and a fellow at the Weatherhead Center for International Affairs at Harvard University. "Who is like that? I had to ask myself, 'Was he really that focused?'"

Over the years, Kagame has distinguished his leadership in numerous ways, among them his single-minded drive for execution. It is one thing to have a vision; indeed, many African leaders start out with a great vision and even better intentions. It is quite another thing for a leader to keep the goals in his or her line of sight and execute against a plan. A leader must be highly capable of driving big-picture results with dogged discipline while demanding individual results from the entire team.

Kagame's unwavering commitment to move Rwanda forward draws comparisons to a corporate CEO, particularly as he stays focused on the vision, pushes for results, and demonstrates decisiveness. Just as strong CEOs understand the levers of their businesses that will improve growth and profitability, Kagame knows what is most important to facilitate the growth and development of Rwanda. "We call him the CEO of Rwanda . . . He runs the country like a business," observed Faustin Mbundu, chairman of the Private Sector Federation, an umbrella organization that represents numerous business associations in the country.

Everyone we asked, from private-sector entrepreneurs to Western business leaders involved in Rwanda, provided the same answer: the economic and social progress realized in Rwanda since the genocide is directly attributable to the leadership of Paul Kagame. Clearly Kagame is a highly skilled motivator of people, leading the turnaround plan for Rwanda as the country has emerged out of human and political bankruptcy.

"Much of the credit must reside with him: his discipline, his focus, his persistence, and his dedication to reversing the old order in Rwanda," said U.S. Assistant Secretary of State for the Bureau of African Affairs Johnnie Carson, who previously served as the national intelligence officer for Africa at the National Intelligence Council, which is charged with advising the U.S. president and policymakers on foreign policy issues. Carson credited Kagame's leadership for achievements such as improved access to health care, increased agricultural production, and the focus on information technology as a catalyst to drive development and establish a new economy in a small landlocked country with limited natural resources. Kagame, he observed, has demonstrated abilities to "ensure that the country's future is strong, based on its primary resource—its people."

Such praise begs the questions: how did a military general in charge of an army that overthrew a corrupt government and stopped the genocide transform into a free-market advocate who seeks to develop the human capital of his country as a way of attracting foreign investment? How did he come to embrace and even embody the vision to transform a society based on subsistence agriculture into a technology-driven marketplace? The answers lie in the nature of the man himself.

The attribute we heard most frequently was Kagame's discipline. During his days in the Rwandan Patriotic Front (RPF), he trained his body to require little food or sleep. Today that quality is evident in his physical appearance, commanding presence, and habit of working late into the night. For his staff and close associates, the last phone call of the night is likely to be from him. No matter how early in the morning someone has reviewed the international news, he has read it already.

Associates also described him as both feared and revered. The fear stems from the well-known consequences of breaking the law. Some former associates and even friends have gone to jail for corruption. Kagame greatly disdains corruption because of its devastating effect on building trust and legitimacy in government. Early on in his presidency, people who were accustomed to receiving $10,000 in spending money for a European trip quickly found out the rules had changed. As one Western observer noted, "With Kagame you'd better be afraid to break the rules." Today, the country's "zero corruption" policy is a hallmark of its leadership and governance. (Just outside the parking lot at Kigali airport, one of the first sights visitors see upon arriving in the country is a sign reading: "Investment yes. Corruption no.")

There is also a steely toughness to Kagame. Although soft-spoken and amiable with us, he showed an unshakable resolve on issues such as Rwanda's right to self-determination and of-fered no apologies or explanations. He shared good-naturedly the frustration of his communication staff, which sometimes tries, for the sake of public relations, to at least get him to smile for the camera during interviews. But there was no joking in his tone when he said, "I am what I am. I have nothing to hide. I will tell them what I think, take it or leave it."

In that directness, we saw the attributes that others spoke of when recalling episodes during and immediately after the war. "He has extraordinary courage," Defense Minister James Ka-barebe, who served with Kagame in the RPF, recalled. "I don't know where it comes from . . . But he knows how to make deci-sions when nobody is making them."

As for being revered, Kagame is widely viewed among Rwan-dans as a role model who has given people a reason to be proud of themselves and their country. "Rwanda today is important and meaningful," the president remarked. "In the past, no one valued it. But today, the most important difference is that people have come to value themselves and to value others. They are not secondary; they are not second-rate. That is the difference between then and now, and it has changed Rwanda forever."

Eugene Haguma, CEO of Horizon Group, a Rwandan pri-vate equity venture that invests military pension funds, recalled one of Kagame's early directives: for Rwandans to improve the cleanliness and appearance of the country. At the time, with so many problems facing them—including extreme poverty—cleanliness seemed like an odd priority. "We thought that you needed to be educated first, or to be wealthy first, before you could think about being clean," Haguma explained. "But he did not see it that way. Cleanliness was about people being confident in themselves." Cleanliness, orderliness, and organization—which Kagame experienced in his household growing up, despite the poor conditions of refugee camps—do not require money. Moreover, they are the foundation of self-worth and self-respect, from which wealth creation becomes possible.

The older generation, which experienced such unspeakably hard times, sees evidence of Kagame's leadership in such things as improved access to health care and a higher quality of life, even at the lowest socioeconomic levels. The president is also viewed as the champion of the national reconciliation effort. "If you ask an elderly lady, as I have, the question, 'Why would you forgive the perpetrator who murdered your husband [during the genocide] and allow that person to move into the house next to you?' she will say, 'God would not have enabled me to survive in order to hate.' The second thing she will say is, 'The president has asked me to do it,'" commented Fairbanks.

Another attribute that distinguishes Kagame's leadership is his consistent focus on the future. Although he is firmly grounded in reality, his vision is not limited or impaired by how things are today. Dr. Richard Sezibera, who served as a field doctor in the RPF and then became Rwanda's minister of health from 2008 until April 2011, recalled that Kagame exhibited this foresight as far back as 1994. "Everybody else was focused on the destruction. He consistently focused on what the country would become," observed Sezibera, who today is secretary general of the East African Community.

With ambitious plans often comes impatience. No matter how much progress is made, more is always needed. Meeting goals on time is the least that's expected; exceeding them or accomplishing them ahead of schedule is what Kagame really wants. With so much to be accomplished, everything becomes a priority because all of it—from health care to education, private sector development to expanding energy generation—must be done well and quickly. Mistakes can be forgiven, but incompetence is inexcusable. Kagame, it's clear, doesn't suffer fools lightly.

Another facet of Kagame's leadership is his openness to innovation and eagerness to draw new ideas and feedback from others, both inside and outside the country. He is collaborative and inclusive, seeking out multiple sources of information before making decisions. "He runs his ideas by a number of people. Consensus is important to him. He wants input always," Foreign Minister Louise Mushikiwabo commented.

Over the years, Kagame has met with numerous CEOs and business leaders, including Howard Schultz of Starbucks and Jim Sinegal of Costco, both of whom have become supporters of the country and major buyers of Rwandan coffee, and Jamie Dimon of JPMorgan Chase, which supported the first-ever financial analyst training conducted in Rwanda, part of a larger effort to develop professional talent in the country. Other corporate leaders with whom Kagame has met include Rob Glaser of RealNetworks, Eric Schmidt of Google, Riley Bechtel of Bechtel Construction, Warren Stephens of investment bank Stephens

Inc., John Tyson of Tyson Foods, Mike Duke and Rob Walton of Walmart, David O'Reilly of Chevron, and Steve Forbes of Forbes Media. They are part of a network of "well-placed friends," which *Fast Company* described as the country's "one abundant asset" in luring private investors, training new managers, building an economy that can compete globally, and ending its need for foreign aid.[2]

When he meets these leaders, Kagame's message is always clear: Rwanda is open for business and welcomes foreign investment in a free-market environment. "Things won't happen without investment, without capital coming in. And that capital must benefit those who invest and also those who are on the ground where the investment is being made," Kagame said. Investment, as he sees it, is the antidote to overreliance on aid and donation, which do not empower people to help themselves. Instead, people are left in a kind of development limbo, which Kagame called "neither dead nor alive." On the other hand, the infusion of capital to launch an industry or start a business reenergizes society and helps people realize their potential. "When capital comes in, people who had been sitting on the roadside start doing things, rather than expecting always to benefit from the generosity of others," he added.

To encourage investment and development, Kagame has relied on the resources and brainpower of his Presidential Advisory Council, (PAC): a group of business, government, academic, and religious leaders (Rwandan and international) who act as ad-hoc advisers. The PAC, which convenes twice a year (in April in Kigali and in September in New York in conjunction with the United Nations General Assembly session), was officially launched in September 2007. Just as corporate CEOs rely on strong boards of directors for advice and counsel, Kagame has turned to those who have the knowledge, expertise, and perspective that Rwanda needs in every facet of its development.

Clet Niyikiza is a Rwandan who left his country in 1983. After receiving a PhD in theoretical mathematics from the University of Indiana, he spent much of his career in the pharmaceutical industry, including Syntex Corp., Eli Lilly, and GlaxoSmithKline, where he was a vice president and medicine development leader for oncology. In all those years, he never returned to Rwanda. "After the tragedy of the genocide, I was left with a sense that I needed to focus on things that actually protect life, instead of taking it. And so I was in pharmaceutical research," he told us. He focused on cancer research, contributing to several significant discoveries. During that time, his wife of 25 years, who was also Rwandan, was diagnosed with a rare form of lymphoma that quickly metastasized to her brain. Before she died, she asked Niyikiza to promise he would return to Rwanda one day.

In September 2006, just as he was leaving for a business trip to Tokyo, Niyikiza received a call from Rwanda's ambassador to the United States, asking if he could meet with Kagame in Morristown, New Jersey. With about a 45-minute window before he had to leave for Newark to catch his flight, Niyikiza agreed. The meeting was brief, but at the end, Kagame urged him to come to Rwanda. Niyikiza told him, "Mr. President, if you want to have a future, you have to start early. I didn't have a future there; I found it here." Kagame made one final appeal: "You're welcome to visit home."

Niyikiza left for the airport with a feeling that perhaps it was time for some soul searching. As a scientist, he recognized that the variables had changed; it was time to reevaluate his assumptions about Rwanda. "I concluded that this president was very different from the folks I was used to," he told us. "First, he cares for his people instead of his pockets. Second, you could sense a genuine desire to take the country to a different place. I started reading more and asking questions. Eventually I said, 'This guy is going somewhere.'"

In March 2007, Niyikiza traveled back to Rwanda to see relatives and familiarize himself anew with his homeland. As he was leaving, Niyikiza received a call from Kagame's office. Instead of taking the night flight out of Kigali to Brussels, would he accompany the president, who was headed to San Francisco via London? En route to the United Kingdom, the two men discussed many topics, including how to channel the efforts of the many "friends of Rwanda" who championed the country. That conversation led to the idea of the PAC (Niyikiza was quick to point out the concept did not originate with him), which found support with others, including Chicago businessman and financial services entrepreneur Joe Ritchie, a long-time supporter of Rwanda. Ritchie told us over a dinner at his house in Kigali, to which he travels frequently from his home in Chicago, "There is nothing here that, in principle, can't happen."

The PAC streamlined the process by which Rwanda could tap into the energy and ideas of some of its most influential supporters, who include former UK Prime Minister Tony Blair; Scott Ford, former CEO of Alltel and founder of Rwanda Trading Company; Michael Roux of Australia, chairman of Roux International; Michael Porter, Harvard Business School professor and expert on competitive strategy; Doug Shears, executive chairman of ICM Australia; and Rev. Rick Warren, founder of Saddleback Church in California and author of *The Purpose Driven Life*; as well as Niyikiza, Ritchie, Fairbanks, Miller, and several others. Rwandans who serve on the PAC include the ministers of foreign affairs, finance, and local government; the governor of the National Bank of Rwanda; the ambassador to the United States; and Bishop John Rucyahana.

Among those who joined the PAC soon after its founding was former Stephens Inc. investment banker and entrepreneur Dale Dawson, who had also served as a KPMG national director and CEO of TruckPro, which he sold to AutoZone. The founder and CEO of Bridge2Rwanda and ISOKO Institute, which promote foreign investment, entrepreneurship, servant leadership, and education in the country, Dawson quickly decided that the transformation that occurred in Rwanda was directly attributable to Kagame's leadership. "It was his judgment, will, energy level, and persuasiveness," Dawson said. "He reassigned priorities and put pressure on certain areas to get results. It's hard to argue that security is more important or that education is less important. It's all important, and President Kagame knows that."

At a PAC meeting in April 2008, Fairbanks and Niyikiza sat next to each other at lunch, brainstorming about how they could respond to an observation Kagame made earlier that day: in order to expect better outcomes, Rwanda would have to do things differently. One of the possibilities they discussed was Rwanda investing in a promising new biopharmaceutical company, Merrimack Pharmaceuticals, in which Fairbanks had been a small investor early on. Given Niyikiza's expertise as a well-respected, senior pharmaceutical executive, he could conduct due diligence and provide guidance as a private citizen, with all the appropriate nondisclosure restrictions. When they approached Kagame with the idea, the president was eager to pursue it. Although Merrimack management was reluctant at first, fearing it was too risky for a developing country to put a portion of its pension funds into a biopharmaceutical company, Kagame was undeterred. As Fairbanks observed, here was a leader who had led outnumbered fighters to victory to end civil war and stop a genocide; how could someone tell him what was risky?

Rwanda eventually invested $16 million in Merrimack Pharmaceutical, which is based in Cambridge, Massachusetts. After retiring from GlaxoSmithKline, Niyikiza was recruited to become executive vice president of Merrimack, which focuses on treatments of cancer and other serious diseases. According to its filing with the Securities and Exchange Commission for a planned initial public offering (IPO) expected to take place in 2012, Merrimack has four targeted therapeutic oncology treatments in development and a fifth expected to enter clinical development. For Rwanda, a successful IPO would provide a healthy return on its investment. Regardless of the outcome, the investment demonstrates Kagame's willingness to think beyond the status quo and take what he deems is an appropriate risk.

Kagame sets aggressive goals, develops processes to review and assess progress, gives continual and candid feedback, and lets people know when they have not cleared the bar. His staff is motivated to perform at the highest level, sometimes stretching the boundaries of their individual capabilities. Unlike the common image of government jobs as being cushy, low-stress positions, the reality in Rwanda is the opposite: these people work incredibly hard. Kagame's team, especially the ministers and others in key positions, bring both impressive credentials and a deep passion for serving their country.

One of the most important qualities he looks for in his staff members, Kagame said, is character. "It always comes first," he said. Yet character alone is not enough. In Rwanda, because there is an acknowledged experience gap as institutions, policies, and procedures are still being put in place, the marriage of character and ability is crucial. "You cannot just have character and good behavior and not be knowledgeable," Kagame added. "That's why we train people. Many of us have been trained on the job."

Kagame is also known for moving people around a lot, from one ministry to another. In some instances, it is to develop people and provide more experience; in others it is to shake things up a bit. "I'm sure it confuses many people, but there is a tendency that you have to deal with which had a lot to do with the politics [in the past]," he explained. "People tended to equate themselves with the institutions they are responsible for. They saw themselves as there to stay, but they were not thinking in terms of the institution. They were thinking of themselves. Then they become an institution unto themselves."

Instead of staying at one ministry for an extended period of time, especially if it means working with close associates, friends, or even relatives, ministers are moved to take on new responsibilities, with different staffs to motivate and manage. As they face new challenges, they develop new, broader skills and abilities. It is akin to the processes within large businesses that develop the breadth and depth of a management team. It also underscores that institutions are built on the principle of service. As Kagame explained, "Government officials start saying, 'I belong to commerce or I belong to finance, but I am serving the country.'"

When a leader is a relentless driver, the perennial risk is that his people will burn out. For Kagame's team, the challenge is keeping pace with a very strategic leader who also dives deep into the details. The onus is on his team members to do the same; expectations are high. Moreover, because Kagame has such a strong presence and is always in control, some people find him intimidating. Luckily, within this demanding environment, he shares credit and celebrates the accomplishments of others, which serves to motivate everyone around him.

As for his own accomplishments, Kagame was dubbed "the star of a new Africa recast as a place of growth and opportunity," by *Time* magazine in 2010. Kagame, the article states, "has presided over Rwanda's stunning rebirth." It cited roads, schools, running water, and phones that are widespread; the decline in disease; and the rises in literacy and life expectancy. Kagame's track record in Rwanda even led the United Nations to name him in June 2010 the cochair of a new panel on ending world poverty.

The article also acknowledged another view of Kagame and his leadership as portrayed largely in the Western press, due to the arrest of political opponents in the run-up to the September 2010 election in which Kagame was reelected by a landslide. As *Time* noted, Kagame's critics "have made the inevitable comparison of him to the continent's notorious Big Men." The article quoted Kenneth Roth, head of Human Rights Watch, who stated, "We have no problems acknowledging [Kagame] has done positive things. But we question whether the world should be closing its eyes to dictatorship."

Yet, as the *Time* article also pointed out, Rwanda "is not an easy place to explain."[3] It has been only 18 years since the genocide and a dozen since the country stabilized and stopped the insurgency that threatened national security. There is the real possibility that old tensions in the country, despite the best gains made in reconciliation and unification, make Rwanda a powder keg. The Kagame administration has defended its actions for jailing some political opponents on the grounds they allegedly used their platforms as a means to re-ignite ethnic hatred, in violation of the country's anti-genocide ideology laws. In an interview with *Newsweek,* Foreign Minister Mushikiwabo countered the allegation that the RPF, as the party in power, intimidates the opposition: "That portrayal is inaccurate. The fact that Rwanda [had] four presidential candidates [in the 2010 election] is nowhere to be seen in international media. We see that those political aspirants who tend to be on the extreme in terms of ethnic discourse, in terms of what should happen with the country, are the ones who are getting the attention."[4]

Even *Time* conceded that Kagame's abolishment of the death penalty, release of prisoners to participate in reconciliation, decentralization of the government, giving of seats in his cabinet to the opposition, and stand against African homophobia are "hardly the actions of a tyrant."[5]

In our interviews with Kagame, and in conversations with dozens of people who live and work in the country, there was no evidence of the president as an iron-fisted dictator. Strong, yes; strongman, no. For one, Kagame is committed to building institutions to secure smooth transitions and continuity in the future, which will make Rwanda less reliant on any one individual, including him. Furthermore, the overblown ego of a despot is not there; Kagame does not like talking about himself. "I am more comfortable with other people talking about my weaknesses and strengths rather than me talking about them," he told us. The only talent he acknowledged in any particular way was his ability to read people. "I just need a day to work with people to understand them. I only have to look someone in the eye, and later on when we part, I can say 'this is a good person' or 'this one I don't know about.' Reading people is my passion," he added. It is also a sign of a highly intuitive leader.

Finally, while Kagame is very capable and has never doubted his own ability, he was initially reluctant to step into the spotlight. "I have always been hesitant to lead, which is different from doubting my ability," Kagame explained. "There have been times when others have said, 'Who is going to do this?' and I would stay back. I would not say, 'It's me; I am the one to do it.' I have always been reluctant to be there first, but whenever I am there, I do my best."

The first time Kagame refused to take a leadership role was after the death of RPF commander Fred Rwigema. As the new leader of military operations, Kagame was under pressure to become head of the RPF organization as well, which he refused on principle. Someone else had been appointed vice chairman under Rwigema. The right thing to do, Kagame told his colleagues, was to find the vice chairman and determine if he was willing to serve as RPF chair. The second time was when he declined the presidency postgenocide. As major general of the RPF, Kagame had stated publicly he had no interest in a postwar political career. He demonstrated that conviction when he refused, to the dismay of many people in the RPF, to become president and instead favored someone who was better known to Rwandans within the country. Even though that person proved to be the wrong choice (because of allegations of corruption), Kagame did not regret his decision. "Everybody turned to me and said, 'We told you.' They held me responsible for two things: one, that they had told me this was the wrong person and, second, that they had told me I should be the president and bear the responsibility . . . But the premise on which I made the decision is still right today, although maybe I [backed] the wrong person. The premise still makes sense to me."

Clearly Kagame has deviated from the path of other leaders on the continent, including his neighbor, Yoweri Museveni, who became president of Uganda in January 1986 following a military coup (as related in Chapter 2) and remains in office today. Kagame's administration is very much aligned with a servant leadership model, which holds that leaders must devote themselves first and foremost to the best interest of their constituents, not the other way around. (In the corporate world, it declares that a CEO should stay focused on what is right for shareholders and other important stakeholders.) Despite the adulation he receives in a country that he in many ways personifies, Kagame has managed to resist the common pitfall of letting power overwhelm him. "What happens sometimes is that people get riches that they don't expect to have and they get power. They control so much, and this goes deep into their heads," Kagame reflected. "They get drunk with it."

Much of his resolve comes, no doubt, from his famous self-discipline and restraint, which are the products of his upbringing and early experiences. But personality and character also play an important part. "There is an image out there of him as a very cold, almost military 'do as I say' kind of a person, and he's not," Foreign Minister Mushikiwabo observed. "He's actually very generous with his time . . . If you could see how many people he receives in his office here every day . . . But because of his military background as a general, people lose sight of that human side of him."

Truly one of the defining outcomes of Kagame's leadership is the motivation and empowerment of the Rwandan people, from rural farmers who have increased crop yields to feed their families and sell the excess to a new generation of entrepreneurs in a knowledge-based economy. As Finance Minister John Rwangombwa observed, "He is able to drive most of the country to believe we can do big things, when we thought before that we couldn't do anything." He credits Kagame's long-term vision and thinking for creating a "culture in which nothing is impossible."

Rwanda's growing pains are far from over. But if its most recent years are indicative of its future, the country is positioned to do well, indeed, provided it can maintain peace and stability and foster economic development for all. If that happens, decades from now people will point to one person who made all the difference at a critical time, a visionary leader who empowered others to join his cause: Paul Kagame.

6

THE RWANDA MODEL

In a tiny rural neighborhood known as an *umudugudu,* a shiny slab of sheet metal caught the midday sun. The flash of silver stood out among the mostly one- and two-room houses in the settlement known as Sunzu in the Northern Province, where typical roofs made of low-quality, locally crafted tile do a passable job of keeping out the torrential rains. In other, less rainy parts of the country, roofs have been commonly made of thatch, which is being phased out by the government because of health hazards associated with leaking, dampness, mold, and the insects that live in the grassy material. More than any architectural statement, the new roof on this modest house in an economically disadvantaged area sent an important message about Rwanda: someone in the *umudugudu* had come into some money to afford that piece of corrugated metal sheeting, perhaps by selling part of a harvest or maybe a goat, which was beyond what the family needed to feed themselves. In a country chronically gripped by poverty, the shining metal roof is an undeniable sign of progress at the lowest socioeconomic tier.

In a world of failed economic models, Rwanda stands apart. Through strong leadership, decentralization to empower the grassroots, free markets, private sector development, managing and aligning the activities of nongovernmental organizations (NGOs) with the Rwandan government's priorities, and active courting of foreign direct investment—all enhanced by cultural values and traditions—Rwanda has become a model for the developing world. The Rwanda model contrasts starkly with countries like Haiti, which was devastated by an earthquake in January 2010. A year later, *Time* magazine declared the Caribbean nation was "still a basket case," with more unemployment, destitution, and foreign dependence than ever, in spite of $11 billion in donor pledges.[1]

The West has given more than a trillion dollars in aid to Africa over the past four decades. But as former Goldman Sachs banker Dambisa Moyo, author of *Dead Aid,* told *Fast Company* magazine, "No nation has ever attained economic development by aid. It's just not productive." Even worse, the magazine pointed out, aid can be destructive if the money finds its way into the pockets of corrupt leaders or is squandered inefficiently. "Millions of people end up hooked on handouts," *Fast Company* added.[2]

That's not the path Rwanda has chosen. President Paul Kagame preaches a gospel of economic self-reliance, turning the country, especially the younger generation, into a nation of believers. Rwanda also boasts a willing cadre of civil servants to execute the plans and objectives as espoused in Vision 2020. Of course, Rwanda's progress has not been made in isolation; they've had significant help from the outside, including NGOs who provide assistance, training, and know-how. But rather than pouring money into their own pet projects, NGOs in Rwanda must conform to the government's agenda and priorities. Otherwise, an NGO is likely to find its help is no longer wanted.

Implementing the Rwanda model of economic development has required more than government action. It demanded a complete change in perspective, all the way down to the local level. "The thinking here was totally different," Kagame told us. Previous regimes made people completely dependent on the government. Regular handouts from above, including jobs or admissions to the university, reinforced corruption as well as ethnic discrimination and regional favoritism, which in turn stoked the fires of hatred that erupted with the genocide.

From a purely economic point of view, when people are not productive, the government cannot draw resources from them, such as tax revenues. Then, all the government can do is to rely on foreign aid. "[When that happens] the government has nothing because it cannot get anything from the people," Kagame explained. "It only ends up begging donors to come in, and then they provide everything. Then the donors [in effect] become the government."

But not on Kagame's watch. He has called dependence on foreign aid dehumanizing and believes Rwanda can do for itself. As he told a group of international reporters in Kigali in November 2011, "We have benefited a lot from aid and we still get aid, but our ambition is . . . to need less or no aid. That is our ambition, meaning that [in] time we will be people who can provide for ourselves and stand on our own."[3]

The only way to cut dependence on foreign aid is private investment from local and foreign business interests, which creates jobs and opportunities—and generates tax revenue. Today, paying taxes (arguably not a favorite activity of citizens anywhere) is celebrated in Rwanda to raise awareness and encourage compliance. The Rwanda Revenue Authority presents certificates each year to the best taxpayers, recognizing those who pay the most (the Rwandan brewery Bralirwa has been a past honoree, along with a foreign-owned telecommunications company) as well as those who are the most compliant.

But it is not enough for economic development to move the needle only at the top. The Rwanda model emphasizes economic growth that is "pro-poor." In order to truly make a difference for the country, growth must be demonstrated in the rural areas, where the vast majority of the country's 10.7 million people live. Admittedly, there is a sharp contrast between Kigali, which has a cosmopolitan flair, and the *umudugudu* of Sunzu, which is very humble (although breathtakingly beautiful, surrounded by emerald green hills and a large lake). That's why the shiny new roof in Sunzu is so important. It is a reminder that in order for Rwanda's sweeping economic plan known as Vision 2020 to achieve its aim, the country's development cannot leave any group or region behind.

Central to Vision 2020 is a program known as the Economic Development and Poverty Reduction Strategy. Simply stated, the more Rwanda grows its economy, the more people must be provided opportunities to better their lives. As the Rwandan government's 2008 Joint Governance Assessment report observed, "Some of the greatest constraints to governance in Rwanda are structural and relate to poverty, low levels of education, insecure livelihoods and shortcomings in infrastructure. All of these factors will need to be addressed not only to raise incomes, but also to generate trust, build unity, consolidate peace and create a longer-term basis for civic participation in the context of a transparent, democratic process."[4]

Building trust, both among people and between people and the government, further facilitates economic development. In Rwanda, the latter kind of trust runs high; the government and the military enjoy approval ratings of 80 to 90 percent. "Trust is an asset to Rwanda. In most countries, a lack of trust is the biggest hidden tax on an economic system. In Rwanda, it's an advantage," observed Michael Fairbanks, who is cofounder of the philanthropic SEVEN Fund, a fellow at the Weatherhead Center for International Affairs at Harvard University, and a member of Kagame's Presidential Advisory Council.

Rwanda has made measurable progress on many fronts: universal health care, compulsory education that is expanding to 12 years, a budding private sector, and an inclusive government in which women occupy positions of authority. As noted in Chapter 1, Rwanda recently announced (verified by international experts) that it has reduced the percentage of its population below the poverty line to 44.9 percent in 2011, from 56.9 percent in 2006. The goal is to reduce it further to about 30 percent by 2020.

The *Los Angeles Times* called the poverty reduction a "remarkable achievement for Rwanda," and reached out to Paul Collier, director of the Center for the Study of African Economies at Oxford University, to comment on the numbers. Asked by the newspaper if there were any doubts about the veracity of the data, Collier stated, "No doubts; I know the economics professor who did the data analysis, and he is highly experienced and painstaking, so it is genuine."

Collier also offered his views on how the poverty reduction came about. One reason, he said, is a rise in world prices for coffee, which is a top export for Rwanda and accounts for about 40 percent of its foreign exchange. Another factor is the country itself. "Rwanda is the nearest that Africa gets to an East Asian style 'developmental state,' where the government gets serious about trying to grow the economy and where the president runs a tight ship within [a] government built on performance rather than patronage."[5]

Rwanda has been deliberate in its pursuit of economic development that mirrors the East Asian "tiger" economies such as those in Hong Kong, Singapore, South Korea, and Taiwan, all of which achieved very high economic growth from the early 1960s through the 1990s. In fact, it has set its sights on becoming the "Singapore of Africa." Its roadmap toward that goal is Vision 2020, a sweeping and ambitious business plan for the country that was adopted by the Rwandan government in July 2000, before the country even had a constitution. Vision 2020 identified six pillars for Rwanda's development: good governance; transformation of agriculture into a productive, high value, and market-oriented sector; development of an efficient private sector; human resources development through education, health, and technology skills; infrastructure development including transportation, energy, water, and information and communications technology (ICT) networks; and promotion of regional economic integration and cooperation.

The first pillar, good governance, recognizes the role of the state in fostering an environment in which human capital development and wealth creation become possible. Today Rwanda is determinedly following a path of decentralization to push authority and accountability down to the local level. Empowering the grassroots means giving people a say in what they need in their local communities—a school building, a clinic, a new road—and the responsibility to get it done. Such inclusion in governance, particularly at the local level, converts people from passive bystanders to stakeholders. With a hand in their own betterment, they are also more likely to support other initiatives like reconciliation and unification. Postgenocide, the interconnectedness of peace and prosperity can never be underestimated.

To understand decentralization, one must be familiar with Rwanda's structure. Today, it has five provinces: Northern, Southern, Eastern, Western, and Kigali, the capital. (Before 2006, there were 12 provinces, vestiges of old regional rivalries that contributed to the genocide.) The provinces are subdivided into districts, which are further broken down into sectors. Below the sector is the local level, or cell, which consists of several *umudugudu*.

Minister of Cabinet Affairs Protais Musoni, who previously served as the minister of Local Government), placed a one-page colored printout on a table in front of us. The graphic showed a series of diamonds and triangles that, on a timeline from left to right, decreased in size and complexity: a visual representation of Rwanda's mission to reduce the number and size of the layers at the top while broadening the base of influence at the local level on the bottom.

The country's governance structure in 2000 was an elongated diamond shape, with a strong central government at the top and the breadth of power and authority resting in the many administrative layers underneath. Only a tiny, narrow line showed the trickle of involvement down to the local level. From 2002 to

2006, the size and shape of the structure changed, with a shrinking central government, fewer administrative layers, and more decision-making authority funneling down to the local level. By 2015, Rwanda's governance will resemble a short, thin triangle, with a small central government at the top, slightly bigger provincial and district levels in the middle, and a broader base at the local cell level.

"In the end, the local level has more responsibility for governance," Musoni stated. "Once you have full ownership of the state within the population, then you get real stability."

In order for decentralization to be effective, skills must be developed. In the public and private sectors alike, human resource development is a critical need. A lack of qualified people to produce results quickly is the weak spot in the Rwanda model. People, particularly in the public sector, may be afraid to make mistakes; therefore, there can be little incentive for them to take initiatives on their own. Hesitancy to make decisions is rooted in the fear of what would happen if they are questioned; if there is even a hint that something done could be interpreted as corrupt or against the rules, they likely would be investigated and then carry the stigma, even if allegations proved false. Rwanda's policy of zero tolerance for corruption is a huge positive for the country, but the unintended consequence can be frustrating delays due to bureaucracy, checks and double checks, and reluctance to make a decision. And it's all too easy to find a loophole or a reason to delay a decision, particularly at the middle and lower levels of government ministries. This inefficiency puts the problems back on the desks of ministers and permanent secretaries, creating a backlog. (One foreign investor, facing an eleventh-hour deadline, told us he had to force the issue by driving to a minister's house one evening in order to procure a signature on a document that had already been approved by multiple parties in the government.) Such delays are frustratingly common when dealing with the public sector. Therefore, Rwanda must continue to push to improve the skill sets of public servants, particularly to support the development of the private sector.

"Rwanda's biggest problem is a human capacity problem. There are not enough people in authority who can get the job done," observed Carter Crockett, an American-born entrepreneur, management scholar, and cofounder of Karisimbi Business Partners, a socially motivated consultancy based in Rwanda that seeks to develop small- and medium-size businesses in Rwanda and elsewhere in East Africa. "You can address some of the human capacity problem with 'formal education,' but a lot of what is needed is learned in the 'school of hard knocks,' which comes with experience. As many of the diaspora come back to Rwanda [particularly those with university degrees], young people often find themselves in positions of immense authority beyond their years. Too few people doing too much work, and without enough qualified people to delegate authority to—that's a common thread across institutions of all types here."

Minister of Infrastructure Albert Nsengiyumva, who assumed his current post in May 2011, is among the highly qualified members of the diaspora who returned to Rwanda. Born in Burundi of parents who had left Rwanda after the 1959 pogroms, Nsengiyumva received a degree from the National University of Burundi and continued his studies in engineering and ICT in the United States and Belgium. Before moving to Rwanda, he worked for the government of Luxembourg at its state computer center, providing technical support as the country centralized its communication systems. By 1997, however, Nsengiyumva decided it was time to move to Rwanda, which he had always considered home though it was personally unfamiliar to him. After working in the ICT sector in Europe, Nsengiyumva took a huge pay cut with a job at the National University of Rwanda as the director of the computer center, earning about $50 per month. Over the course of his Rwandan career, he also worked with the Ministry of Education on several vocational training projects, developing curricula that are responsive to the needs of the country's business sectors.

In becoming the minister of infrastructure, Nsengiyumva took on a huge responsibility encompassing transportation (roads, air, rail) and the all-important energy sector; he also works closely with other ministries on housing, agricultural development, water, and sanitation. With such a big portfolio of projects to oversee, Nsengiyumva recognizes that human capital development is a common concern across all of them. "At the beginning, people thought we could fix it quickly. As time goes on, however, new challenges arise. Even as the economy improves, it brings new challenges," he added. "When you put a system or a facility in place, a new skill is required."

Ann Lineve Wead Kimbrough, an American conducting doctoral research of leadership on post-genocide Rwanda and its impact on the country's development, believes that human capital—an abundant resource in this most densely populated African country—is "the greatest factor to determine future and sustained economic progress in Rwanda. There is great potential in harnessing the natural opportunities in such a great number of people. The challenge is to continue to increase the knowledge base of Rwandans."

Kimbrough, who was recently named dean of Florida A&M University's School of Journalism and Graphic Communication, analyzed multiyear qualitative and quantitative data that suggest a better educated Rwandan population will help the country continue its economic growth and development.[6]

Fortunately, Rwanda recognizes this need and has welcomed partners who are interested in building its human resource capacity, particularly within the public sector. The assistance Rwanda values the most is training—giving high-potential people the hands-on development and experience they need to become more competent. "The primary problem for Africa now is not traditional aid, but governance in terms of efficiency and getting things done. That's the great problem," said former British Prime Minister Tony Blair, who is also the founder of the Africa Governance Initiative. Luckily, this problem also plays to Kagame's strengths: his relentless desire to drive implementation and create efficiency.

In any large organization, including governments and multinational corporations, the challenge is to ensure the message at the top travels down throughout the organization. To address that gap, Blair's initiative has partnered with the Rwandan government to promote the development of governance skills. As part of the government of Rwanda's project, known as the Strategic Capacity Building Initiative, 41 international experts are being brought in to train the next generation of Rwandan public servants. As of late 2011, 150 young Rwandans were being trained to help the government improve its delivery against priorities in development and self-sufficiency: agricultural productivity, energy generation, electrification, and increasing investment in the private sector. In the process, these young Rwandans are being prepared for future leadership roles. "We put a team of people alongside people in government," Blair explained. "We are very much focused on implementation skills and how you get things done."

In a May 2012 speech at Stanford University's Graduate School of Business, Blair called on the United States and European nations to use what he called "muscular soft power diplomacy . . . [which] is using our technical expertise, intellectual capital, and experience of what works in government in partnership with African leaders so that African nations can accelerate their development, replace aid with investment, and be masters of their own destiny. This partnership should empower the new generation of politicians, business people, and civic society organisers to create sustainable political, economic, and social growth: sustainable, because they are doing it with our help, not waiting for us to do it for them."[7]

When Blair met with us in New York in late 2011, he had just returned from a conference in South Korea. Reflecting on what he saw in Asia, Blair offered some perspective on Rwanda's aspirations to eventually become a middle-income nation. In the 1960s, he observed, South Korea had a GDP on par with Sierra Leone; today, South Korea is the thirteenth-largest economy in the world, with a GDP that is approaching European standards. The South Korean port of Busan, once just a few old piers, is one of the world's busiest ports. Blair sees the potential for Rwanda to become a similar economic success story one day on the strength of its leadership and governance. "The opportunity is there. This is where someone like President Kagame can be a real role model," he added.

IMIHIGO AND ACCOUNTABILITY

Central to governance in the Rwanda model is accountability. Kagame holds a strict standard for his team, particularly at the ministerial level. Detail-oriented and execution-driven, Kagame keeps close tabs on projects, making sure things get accomplished. Nsengiyumva told us, "On critical issues, he keeps following up. The first concern is always delays."

Establishing a culture of accountability goes hand-in-hand with decentralization. Minister of Local Government James Musoni explained that decentralization begins with sharing information on the local level, to get people in the villages and *umudugudu* to sit down together and identify their needs. "They begin to see what they can do for themselves," he explained.

Districts have limited capacity to raise their own funds through fees and taxes; more than 90 percent of district government revenues come from the central government. Nonetheless, other resources can be tapped at the local level, including labor and materials. Execution, however, requires commitment, turning words into action and plans into projects. In order to foster accountability, Rwanda has turned to a cultural tradition known as *imihigo,* a kind of performance contract that goes back to precolonial times when people would publicly state their goals before tribal elders, and others in the community were then expected to support them. Failure to deliver was seen as a dishonor.

"In the old times, within the circle of chiefs, someone would stand up and say, 'I will achieve this.' The moment he did that, the whole community had to be behind him," Protais Musoni explained. "Today, when a local mayor has committed to his *imihigo,* the community is behind him."

In 2006, the Rwandan government reintroduced the concept of *imihigo* to reinforce governance on the local level with a performance-based approach. Once a year, local mayors and district leaders are obliged to report on the progress made and commit to new goals for the upcoming year. Promoting accountability at the local level strengthens governance and improves transparency; goals and results are publicly recorded.

The Rwandan Joint Governance Assessment, released in 2008, two years after the system of *imihigo* was adopted, lauded the practice for strengthening accountability, monitoring the effectiveness of local government, and fostering results-based management. The system of *imihigos,* it added, has been implemented at the lowest tiers of government—even at the level of the household.[8]

Another factor in the Rwanda model is the development of institutions. As Kagame told the group of visiting international journalists in November 2011, "We want to build strong institutions of good governance—institutions that would outlive all of us."[9] Within these institutions, accountability and transparency are enhanced by systems of checks and balances. For example, "horizontal accountability," such as that between branches of government, provides scrutiny and prevents abuses of power. "Vertical accountability" enhances the commitment between the government and all Rwandans, and solidifies the social contract. "Mutual accountability" exists between Rwanda and aid organizations, whereby the government accounts for the responsible use of funds and donors must support the country's development strategies and not their own agendas. In many ways, the Rwanda model mirrors a large decentralized corporate structure, in which individual strategic business units are accountable for their results, performance, and deliverables.

Accountability and power sharing have been tenets of Rwanda's governance since the beginning. After the Rwandan Patriotic Front's (RPF) victory in 1994, it formed a transitional government known as the Government of National Unity. The RPF joined with four political parties (excluding those linked to the genocide) to establish the government based upon the terms of the Arusha Peace Accord, which had been signed in 1993 in an attempt to end the civil war. As Rwanda drafted a constitution, it engaged in town hall–type discussions. From May 1998 to March 1999, meetings were held almost every Saturday in the presidential compound, with a cross section of Rwandans including political and military leaders, local authorities, university professors, journalists, business people, and religious representatives. At the heart of the discussion was the need to understand the roots of the genocide and prevent the country's violent past from repeating itself.

"We brought in all kinds of people—religious leaders, cabinet members, representatives of political parties—and asked them what they thought. We needed people of different backgrounds to give us different perspectives," Kagame told us.

Elderly people, including those who had been part of previous government regimes as well as those who supported the RPF as refugees, recounted what they remembered about Rwanda in the 1940s and 1950s. "They would sometimes tell us different stories and even had arguments about what happened because they remembered and presented it differently, but we were able to pick up some things from the discussion," Kagame added. "We were the new people. We could interpret and be in the middle."

In 2002 and 2003, Rwanda began the formal process of drafting a new constitution, which marked the end of the post-genocide transition. Rwanda also sought input from the outside world. Rwandan delegates visited the United States, spending time with officials in the federal government and in several states, as well as Europe and other African countries. The objective, Kagame explained, was to gather as much input as possible, filter out what was not applicable or suitable for Rwanda, and identify any elements that could be helpful to achieving Rwanda's mission and vision. "We said, 'This can work for us and our problems,' or 'This won't work for us,' or 'This is new and we need to experiment,'" he explained. In the end, the Rwandan constitution became a document of its own design, bringing together the best of what the world had to offer as well as its own solutions.

Among the lessons learned that are integral to the Rwanda model are the importance of popular participation and consultation, rather than relying on what the government called "expert drafting." The constitution also reflects the country's historical context, such as fighting genocide ideology; eradication of ethnic, regional, and other divisions; and promotion of national unity. Other principles call for equitable sharing of power, governing by rule of law, promoting equality of men and women, social welfare and social justice, and seeking solutions through dialogue and consensus.

Among its achievements in governance, Rwanda boasts of its strides toward gender equality and the participation of women in government. The constitution requires at least 30 percent of positions in decision-making bodies in government be occupied by women. Currently, women account for 56 percent of the Rwandan parliament, making it the highest female representation in parliament in the world. (In the United States, including delegates from the District of Columbia, Guam, and the U.S. Virgin Islands, 92 women served in the One Hundred Twelfth Congress, holding 17 percent of congressional seats.)

"We have some good practices in terms of leadership," Foreign Minister Louise Mushikiwabo said. She stopped short of calling Rwanda a role model for other countries but acknowledged, "We can share what Rwanda has achieved by involving women from the grassroots to the top of the country."

Rwanda's Ministry of Gender and Family Promotion was formed, in part, out of the recognition of the role that women had played in the RPF, not only as organizers and soldiers, but also as supporters. Today, this ministry tracks gains made in the advancement of women and equality for both genders, such as in primary school, which has a net enrollment rate of 95 percent, with slightly more than half being girls. Gains have been made in maternal mortality rates (less than 400 per 100,000 live births in 2010, down from 750 in 2005 and 1,071 in 2000, according to Rwandan government statistics), and laws have been passed against gender-based violence, including the establishment of one-stop centers that offer health, psychosocial, legal, and safe-room assistance for victims. In addition to targeting poverty reduction in general, Rwanda has introduced specific measures for women, such as increasing access to credit, allowing women to own property, and supporting women farmers, who account for much of the agricultural sector.

Dale Dawson, CEO and founder of Bridge2Rwanda and the ISOKO Institute and a member of the Presidential Advisory Council, lauded the accomplishments of microfinance in the country to provide access to capital at the lowest economic tier, especially to women. Dawson is among the founders of Urwego Opportunity Bank, established in 2007 and owned by three Christian non-profit organizations: Opportunity International, World Relief, and Hope International. At Urwego, the average loan is approximately $310, made mostly to women to support a small business that helps them feed their families. More than 98 percent of the 40,000 loans are current, with a delinquency rate of less than 2 percent. (In the United States, a delinquency rate of less than 5 percent is considered very good for a commercial bank.)

"We're not trying to motivate people through Urwego. We only work with those who are already motivated, and there are tens of thousands of hard-working, highly motivated people in Rwanda," said Dawson, who serves on the Urwego board. "All they need is opportunity, some capital, and training. We're not doing anything special for them. We are harnessing the work and the drive that they already have and helping them to make more money with what they are already doing."

Urwego also allows people at the lowest economic level to open a savings account with little or even no money. The current average balance among its 138,000 savings accounts is $80. For subsistence farmers whose only source of cash is when the crops are harvested, savings allow for a cushion during the lean times and keeps money out of the way of temptation (and friends and extended family members) to spend it. "The government and the churches in Rwanda are saying to people, 'Saving is a good thing,'" Dawson explained.

Access to even a small amount of capital increases economic opportunity exponentially. For example, small agricultural co-operatives can be formed to raise chickens or to collect and ship milk. Although Rwanda continues to promote ICT as the country's future, particularly in the medium- and long-term, agriculture will be a major sector, driving economic development with increased productivity and value-added products.

"Our farmer/clients are every bit as savvy and business-minded as the entrepreneurs in the city," said Andrew Youn, founder of One Acre Fund, a U.S.-based NGO that has partnered with the Rwandan government to improve productivity in the agricultural sector. "It's wonderful to see that drive for a better future. That same spark you see in the young university student, you also see in a middle-aged farmer who wants a better life for her children."

Currently, One Acre Fund, which recently expanded its operations from Kenya to Rwanda, works with about 2 to 3 percent of the Rwandan population, or roughly 45,000 families, equivalent to 300,000 people. By the end of the decade, One Acre Fund hopes to have contact with 12 percent of the Rwandan population. "Our families have so much untapped potential," Youn commented. "With a little bit of money and a way to earn more money, they will flourish. They invest in their future. They are commercially minded." His words echoed what we were told by another NGO: it is not necessary to bring all the answers and solutions to Rwanda, but rather to provide tools that enable people to do what they have already been doing, in a bigger, better, and more productive way.

For Rwanda to achieve its economic vision, it must foster private sector–led development, which is embedded in the

Rwanda model. In addition to foreign direct investment in businesses and industries, private sector development relies upon entrepreneurship among Rwandans to open a business, generate income, pay taxes, and provide jobs for themselves and others. As Vision 2020 states, a "vibrant middle class of entrepreneurs" must emerge in the country in order to promote the principles of democracy.

Examples of entrepreneurship abound, from vendors who sell fruits and vegetables or baskets in a marketplace, to the younger generation that is looking for a foothold in Rwanda's economy. For example, Ronald, a 20-year-old Rwandan who speaks excellent English, started a one-man tourism company to drive tourists to destinations around the country and provide commentary on the sights as well as the country's history. But as with so many of Rwanda's current goals, entrepreneurship requires a change of mindset. Prior to 1994, the private sector was virtually nonexistent, and much of the economy was controlled by the state. Therefore, there has not been a strong customer-service mentality in Rwanda, unlike, for instance, Kenya, which has a history and tradition of hospitality.

"One of the challenges is getting people to stop doing business like it's a state-owned company and to think the way that private sector people think," explained John Gara, CEO of the Rwanda Development Board, which began operating in January 2009 as a combination of what had been eight separate government departments. "The private sector mentality is especially important in tourism, getting people who work in these kinds of establishments to think of tourists as some of the most important people."

Identifying the problem, however, is half the battle. Through education and training, the resources and know-how of well-educated diaspora, and borrowed talent from abroad, Rwanda has put together a plan to develop a stronger and more equitable economy in keeping with the goals of Vision 2020. Although it espouses a grand plan for Rwanda, Vision 2020 is also pragmatic, with detailed steps for pursuing goals that, even if they are not fully realized, will still result in measurable progress.

"We have always decided to focus on our problems that we need to address. That is central to our thinking," Kagame told us. "We are also realistic about our situation: we know we don't have as many resources to grow from as other countries, so we have to focus on our major resource, which is our people . . . This discussion and being realistic about it has helped the whole country focus on what needs to be done, step by step."

When Vision 2020 was drafted in 2000, Rwanda was already confident in the foundation it had built by solidifying and stabilizing the country from 1998 to 2000. "We could see that something was beginning to happen," Kagame said. By 2005, the gains were beginning to crystallize, convincing him that "it seemed to be really working according to our plan or even beyond our plan."

Thus the thread that runs through the Rwanda model is a mix of both aspiration and pragmatism—to strive to achieve as much as possible but with a clear-eyed view of the problems that need to be addressed. Given what Rwanda has accomplished, especially in terms of poverty reduction, it seems logical that other countries can learn from its example. As Collier from the Oxford University Center for the Study of African Economies told the *Los Angeles Times,* "If Rwanda can do this well, with all its disadvantages—landlocked, legacy of conflict, no natural resources—other African countries should be able to do even better."[10]

Asked what other countries can learn from Rwanda, Kagame was reluctant to elaborate. "We don't want to tell other people what they can learn. We are doing it for ourselves," he told us. And that, perhaps, is the most valuable lesson of all in the Rwanda model: do for yourself, remain independent-minded and self-determining, and forge strategic partnerships with those who support your vision. That's how a country moves itself forward and instills pride and hope in its people.

Construction in the capital city of Kigali provides visual evidence of a growing economy.

A Rwanda Stock Exchange employee records bids, offers, and sales during a trading session. The Exchange was expected to trade in its white board for an electronic platform later in 2012.

President Paul Kagame, who is serving his second democratically elected term, is credited with much of the economic turnaround and revival in his country.

At a vocational school outside Kigali, youths learn circuitry as part of a curriculum that teaches practical skills, which will make them employable in Rwanda's growing economy.

Children filling jerry cans with water underscore the importance of access to safe drinking water. According to government figures, 74 percent of the population has such access, up from 64 percent in 2006.

A mural on a rural schoolhouse in northern Rwanda captures the dream of a country and a community: peace, unity, prosperity, and education for all children.

Rwandan women
weaving traditional
baskets, which honor
an artistic heritage and
provide entrepreneurial
opportunities.

A woman working in her
field in rural Rwanda, where
approximately 80 percent of the
population is currently supported
by subsistence agriculture.

The Virunga Mountains are home to the endangered silverback mountain gorillas. Every year tourists trek to see the animals.

The natural beauty of the "land of a thousand hills" is displayed in a spectacular panorama.

A young man performs in a traditional Rwandan dance. His long blond headdress represents a lion's mane.

A Rwandan mother proudly shows off her baby. Strides in improving access to health care have improved maternal and infant health and significantly reduced mortality.

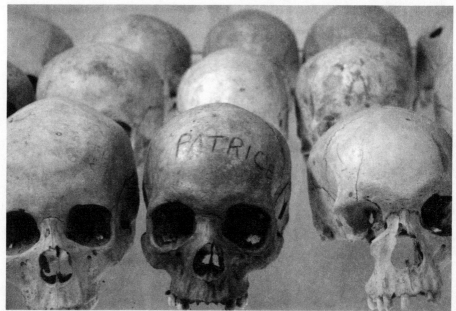

Human skulls at a genocide memorial are a reminder of the one million or more people killed in one hundred days in 1994.

A youth poses with an older woman in his village, representing two faces of Rwanda: the older generation that has known bitter hardships of the past and the younger generation eager to experience the promise of a better future.

Wisdom and perseverance that come from a long and often difficult life are reflected in the faces of these elders.

7

RAISING THE BOTTOM OF THE PYRAMID

On the last Saturday of every month, Rwanda goes to work for itself: clearing land, building classrooms, making roads. On these national days of community work, known as *umuganda*, most shops and businesses are closed. *Umuganda* is a national priority, and everyone is expected to participate. On one particular Saturday, President Paul Kagame and senior government officials showed up in Gasabo District in Kigali province in central Rwanda to plant trees as part of a community project. The president also used the occasion to remind Rwandans that *umuganda* is not just about civic works; it is ultimately about self-sufficiency and dignity.

"This *umuganda* that we are participating in . . . has a purpose—to awaken Rwandans to know that there is a lot we can achieve with the abilities we possess," Kagame told them. Sounding a familiar theme, he reiterated the importance of Rwandans relying on themselves, instead of others, to meet their needs.

"When you are someone else's burden, at one point he will tire of you, drop you hard, and you'll fall apart."[1]

Umuganda is a very tangible way in which Rwanda works at the local level, engaging the grassroots. Just as the country's decentralization policies emphasize local participation in government, other initiatives specifically seek to better the lives of people on the lowest socioeconomic tier. In the process, Rwanda improves security by solidifying support and empowering those most in need. This deep concern for the quality of life at the grassroots stems from the civil war and the fight to end the genocide. Kagame told us: "Nothing would have worked without them." After the genocide, Rwanda was able to put down insurgency from militants and former *genocidaires* who waged cross-border attacks out of what is now the Democratic Republic of the Congo, thanks to the support of local people. "We made them understand that it was in their interest to have security. And, [the country] could not have security without them," Kagame said.

By focusing on people at the lowest socioeconomic tier, the Rwandan government has identified developmental needs, which could cause instability if unmet. Working with international partners and nongovernmental organizations, Rwanda has been making continual progress with major initiatives in three specific areas: agriculture, education, and health care. The list of participants is long, from the World Bank, United Nations' agencies, and the U.S. Agency for International Development (USAID), to the Belgian Development Agency, Japan International Cooperation Agency, and the UK Department for International Development, along with a host of private agencies and humanitarian groups such as Partners In Health and the Clinton Foundation. By focusing on agriculture, health care, and education, Rwanda has been able to make a visible and tangible difference in the lives of its citizens.

"President Kagame has created an environment in which things get done, and that's an important thing," said Ami Desai, foreign policy adviser for former U.S. President Bill Clinton. "As President Clinton has said about the job of being president of the United States, progress depends not on running everything directly yourself, but instead on encouraging and enabling good people and programs to succeed in your country and being supportive of that process in meaningful ways." In Rwanda, a stable and secure environment, emphasis on private sector development, and a supportive and accountable government partner attracts organizations and people who want to help in important and measurable ways. The result is a virtuous cycle in Rwanda, as success breeds more success, all of which elevates the lowest tier of the socioeconomic pyramid.

Clinton, who was in office during the genocide, has taken a special interest in the development of Rwanda. "These people have been through a lot and none of us—most of all me—helped them when they were on the verge of destroying each other. We're undoing that now," Clinton said in a 2007 speech at the TED Conference at which he was honored with the TED Prize for his work in Rwanda, particularly in health care. "And they are so over it, and so into their future. We have a chance to prove that a country that almost slaughtered itself out of existence can practice reconciliation, reorganize itself, and focus on tomorrow, and provide comprehensive quality health care with minimal outside help."[2] Today, the Clinton Foundation and the Clinton Development Initiative, working with local and international partners, champion projects to increase farming yields, develop agribusinesses, and improve the health status of rural Rwandans, especially those afflicted with HIV/AIDS, malaria, tuberculosis, other infectious diseases, and high rates of maternal and infant death.

Yet, in Rwanda, engaging in so many broad initiatives simultaneously is not without its challenges. Gains made in one place trigger new needs. For example, expanding compulsory education from 9 years to 12 intensifies the need for trained teachers, particularly those who can instruct in English. Plans to diversify agriculture and focus on value-added products that could be exported hit the obstacle of high transportation costs. A lack of electricity generation, particularly in rural areas near where crops are grown, thwarts the potential for new processing capacity. As is the case across Rwanda, there is no picking and choosing among initiatives; it must all be accomplished, with greater cooperation among ministries, government agencies, and the Rwandan people themselves.

"It's a country in a hurry. They can't stop the momentum that they've got," one Western observer commented. "It's like the biker who is trying to get to the peak of a summit; you can't let the pack see that you are slipping. You cannot stop moving forward."

Within the many moving parts of Rwanda's development, agriculture is a major focus because of its immediate impact on the population. Gains in crop yields today mean improved food security, better nutrition, and increased income for subsistence farmers whose principal crops include beans, potatoes, plantains, cassava, and sorghum. Over time, a diversified agricultural sector and greater use of mechanization to improve efficiency and yields will hold promise for furthering the country's efforts to expand the overall economy, particularly in the short term, while Rwanda incubates an information and communications technology (ICT) economy for the longer term.

In fact, some observers believe agriculture may continue to be the backbone of Rwanda's economy for the foreseeable future, given that this sector employs the vast majority of people. "In agriculture, I would look at things that have the potential to command a premium after value is added," said Carter Crockett, cofounder of Karisimbi Business Partners, advisers to small- and medium-size companies, including agricultural processors. Among Karisimbi's clients is a tomato processor that packages and distributes tomato paste; its suppliers include more than 4,000 farmers. "When we moved here, we didn't know how to farm tomatoes, but if we focus on the level of the processor, we can learn from local farmers while influencing the entire tomato value chain using what we do have: management expertise."

On the level of the farmer, other efforts are aimed at improving education and training, particularly in the use of modern techniques to improve crop yields, conserve land, and use resources more efficiently. One of the deterrents to improving yield has been traditional land use, with tiny plots and the use of hand tools such as hoes. "When people are educated, they don't want to use the old tools, they want to use new technologies," observed Ernest Ruzindaza, permanent secretary in the Ministry of Agriculture and Animal Resources.

The drive within the agriculture sector has been to encourage farmers to cooperate and combine tiny plots of individually owned land, which may amount to less than a hectare (or a little more than an acre), into larger tracts of 20 hectares or more (roughly 50 acres or more); these can be farmed more efficiently with machines such as tractors that can be hired for plowing or tilling. Other modern farming techniques being introduced include water harvesting, whereby rainwater is collected and used for irrigation, which also helps control erosion; and terracing, which in the "land of a thousand hills" makes more land available for agriculture.

The Rwandan government also supports farmers by buying fertilizer in bulk and distributing it through private sector networks. "That has another element," Ruzindaza explained. "It is supporting not only the farmer but also the private sector to create a network to address the demand."

Andrew Youn, founder of the One Acre Fund, a U.S.-based NGO that works with farmers in Kenya and Rwanda, applauded the Rwandan government's efforts to create "a beneficial agricultural environment" with subsidized fertilizer that is distributed locally. Youn sees the development of the agriculture sector as crucial for Rwanda's future. "Food fuels the economy," he added.

The Clinton Development Initiative, working in partnership with the government, has helped farmers in the poor and dry region of eastern Rwanda buy inputs such as seed and fertilizer in bulk, receive training on advanced farming techniques, negotiate pricing, and apply for fair-trade certification. As a result, maize production more than doubled, compared to the previous year. The bumper crop helped to feed 30,000 people and provided a surplus that raised cash to reduce debt, fund household expenses, and pay school and health care fees. Working with local investment partners, including the Rwandan social security fund administered by Crystal Ventures, the Clinton Development Initiative is also developing agribusinesses, such as a soy processing plant and a coffee roasting and packaging facility, which will eventually be owned locally. Other agricultural initiatives include reforestation and planting fruit and forest trees; the carbon credits from these trees may eventually be monetized and the proceeds returned to the local farmers.

Of all the agricultural programs, the public favorite is the *Girinka* program, otherwise known as "One Cow Per Poor Family." The program, which was initiated in 2006, gives a dairy cow to every poor household to increase milk production, improve nutrition, and to provide manure for soil fertility. In Rwandan culture, where ownership of cows means security and status, the gift of cows to poor families is powerful and symbolic. "The importance of the cow is rooted in cultural attachment," Foreign Minister Louise Mushikiwabo explained. "The value of the cows is much more than money, because it makes people feel that this is part of their culture and tradition. At the same time, you can see the economic benefit of owning a cow, which gives milk and manure, so you are achieving good nutrition and improving agriculture." Further, as milk production increases, collection centers are being established around the country, which is a boost for new agriculture entrepreneurs.

The *Girinka* program also has a unique community-building component. A poor farmer who receives a cow from the government is expected to give the calf it produces to a neighbor. In the first five years of the program, cows were distributed to 150,000 households, and distribution is expanding with help from NGOs and the private sector. The Private Sector Federation, for example, donated 300 million Rwandan francs (equivalent to about US$500,000) to support the *Girinka* program. Faustin Mbundu, chairman of the federation, told us the plan was to double that donation. "Then someone who is poor knows that the business community is helping him," he added.

The Rwandan government is also encouraging farmers to diversify crops, including growing more maize, which ranks second only to sorghum among cereals grown in the country, and third among all crops, according to the Rwanda Agricultural Research Institute. Traditionally, maize was grown mostly in the highland regions, but more recently it has expanded to other areas, including mid-altitudes and semi-arid locales. Maize is also easy to store, making it an important safeguard against crop failure and hunger.

Minimex, a privately owned company, operates a $10 million corn processing plant on the outskirts of Kigali. In early 2012, the plant had been operating initially at only partial capacity. Nonetheless, Minimex chairman Félicien Mutalikanwa spoke confidently about making continued inroads into the Rwandan market, including with sales of product to Bralirwa, the Rwandan brewery. Much of the Minimex corn supply has come from Tanzania and Uganda. But as Rwandan farmers grow more maize and embrace the idea of selling to a large company under contract, Minimex will source more locally, particularly from farming cooperatives.

Among the most unusual crops in Rwanda is pyrethrum, a flowering plant that acts as a natural insecticide. Horizon Sopyrwa, which has been owned by the Rwandan investment company Horizon Group since 2007, processes pyrethrum and accounts for about 5 percent of the world's capacity for extract. The company has about 5,600 hectares (about 13,800 acres) dedicated to pyrethrum cultivation in the Northern Province. "Rwanda is only one of six sources of pyrethrum in the world," said Eugene Haguma, CEO of Horizon Group. "Our ambition is to be the number one producer in the world."

Another important area in agriculture is export promotion, which for Rwanda has meant coffee and tea, accounting for 48 percent of the country's export earnings. After Rwandan tea won awards at an international show held in Mombasa, Kenya in 2011, the Ministry of Agriculture stepped up efforts to increase tea production, working with both farmers and the private sector to encourage investment in these operations. In coffee, the private sector has established additional coffee washing stations, where coffee beans are processed to remove the outer hull, resulting in a value-added product. In 2011, Rwanda earned a record $75 million from coffee exports, compared with $56 million a year earlier, thanks to higher international prices and stronger demand for Rwandan beans.[3]

A recent entrant to the coffee market is Rwanda Trading Company. Established by Scott Ford, an American telecommunications executive who was CEO of Alltel before it was sold to Verizon, Rwanda Trading Company has improved the marketing of Rwandan coffee worldwide and increased the price paid to farmers. Ford knew nothing about the coffee business before Rwanda Trading Company. "I grew up drinking Folgers," he laughed. "I didn't know that there was someone known as a coffee snob."

He focused on this export crop for one simple reason: it accounted for 40 percent of the external dollars raised by foreign exchange. As a member of Kagame's Presidential Advisory Council, Ford concluded that investing in a company could improve foreign exchange and the livelihood of people at the bottom of the socioeconomic pyramid, thus contributing to Rwanda's economic development goals while also serving as a test case for direct foreign investment (as will be discussed further in Chapter 9). While studying the coffee business literally from the ground up—from who owns the land and the trees to who owns the beans to how they are processed and sold—he discovered an important facet of market dynamics: the coffee business in Rwanda had been dominated by two large buyers. Ford saw that with three buyers, even if the new entrant only bought 10 or 20 percent of the crop, the entire market would be repriced in favor of the individual farmer.

Rwanda Trading Company was launched in 2009 as a for-profit Rwandan coffee exporter, selling to buyers in the United States and Europe, including boutique roasters who command a premium product. Rwanda Trading's parent company, Westrock Coffee, also operates a coffee roaster in Arkansas, which sells product to Walmart and has a private label offering through Sam's Club. What this means for the coffee farmers in Rwanda is more demand, a higher income, and greater transparency in pricing. To ensure transparency, contracts between suppliers and buyers—the farmers and the aggregators, the aggregators and the washing stations—are based on world market prices. "It's designing a compensation system," Ford explained.

In addition to promoting coffee and tea exports, the Ministry of Agriculture is investigating opportunities for other value-added products. One example is highland roses, which could potentially be grown year-round because of Rwanda's pattern of two rainy seasons a year. "We want to put a lot of effort into horticulture. It is an opportunity that can create a big source of income for the population and also contribute to the export earnings of the country," Ruzindaza said. "That will be a big priority."

In landlocked Rwanda, transportation challenges exist at every turn, escalating the cost of imported goods and hampering the competitiveness of Rwandan exports. Although these problems are complicated, Rwanda is addressing them with an integrated approach, weaving together agriculture, energy, and transportation. "All these issues come together around agriculture," Ruzindaza said.

The interconnectedness of Rwanda's development is most evident at the lowest tier because of the magnitude of the needs. While improving agriculture addresses pressing needs such as food security and farming income, in the longer term the economy will need to be diversified, with a more robust private sector of entrepreneurs and foreign direct investment. Here, education is crucial to prepare future generations of Rwandans who cannot support themselves off the land. This education also enhances social and political stability, now that it is available to everyone rather than just the country's elite. The illiteracy rate pre-genocide was about 50 percent, and the country only had one university. Today, as noted, Rwanda boasts a primary net enrollment rate of over 95 percent, with girls and boys attending equally, and more than 20 institutions of higher learning.

A 2009 report on education in Rwanda, from public policy think tanks Civic Enterprises and the Hudson Institute, declared, "There are many reasons to be optimistic about Rwanda's prospects for developing a strong education system. The Rwandan government has demonstrated its commitment to education by making education the largest area of federal spending . . ."[4] Indeed, Rwanda commits more than a quarter of its budget to education, thus spending more on the development of the next generation of all Rwandans than it does on defense or any other area of federal spending.

Emphasis on education goes hand-in-hand with Rwanda's policies of reconciliation and unification of the country without ethnic labels or divisions. Pre-genocide, discrimination in schools was common, and students were forced to identify themselves by their ethnic background. During the genocide, schools closed immediately, disrupting education. In September 1994, just two months after the genocide, schools reopened. "The damage done to the educational system during the genocide was extreme, but the experience also galvanized the country around reform, leading to major changes and new investments in the education sector," the Civic Enterprises–Hudson Group report stated.[5]

Sharon Haba, a graduate of Texas A&M University ("I'm a proud Aggie," she laughed), is the permanent secretary in the Ministry of Education. Articulate and thoughtful, she has a passion for education, which she sees as both an individual and collective responsibility. Parents and students are responsible for ensuring attendance, as is the community—in the spirit of *umuganda*. "The schools are there, the teachers are there, the textbooks are there. If you don't send your child to school, someone else holds you accountable," Haba explained.

Within education, the number one challenge is fluency in English. In 2008, the Rwandan Parliament mandated that, starting in fourth grade, all students must be taught in English rather than French or Kinyarwanda. "I really want to have our teachers and students able to communicate well in English. We are getting there slowly, but we know we have a long way to go," Haba said. "If I had $100 to spend, I would put $70 into English."

The second priority, Haba said, is teacher training, in both quantity and quality of available teachers. The need for teachers is so acute, the Ministry of Education is looking to recruit college graduates with majors in other subject areas and then train them to teach. Teachers are also recruited from other English-speaking countries in the region.

The third priority is vocational training, which offers opportunities for students who are not university-bound to learn job skills. "We want to make sure no one is left behind," said Janvier Gasana, deputy director general for the Rwanda Education Board. Currently, about 55 percent of students pursue a general education, while another 40 percent receive technical and vocational training, and the remaining 5 percent are sent to teacher training college. The goal is for 60 percent of students to be in some kind of technical or vocational training by 2017, but finding enough qualified English-speaking teachers, particularly in technical subjects, remains an obstacle. "Technical education needs a lot of investment. We still have gaps, but we are trying to fill those gaps," Gasana added.

At the Nyanza Technical School in the Ruhano sector in the Southern Province, about 60 kilometers from Kigali, some 3,000 students, both boys and girls, learn trades such as electronics, telecommunications, automotive, construction, and public works. Classrooms were modest, but very clean and well organized, and students received hands-on training. In the electronics lab, students worked on resistors and capacitors; in another workshop, students learning automotive electronics tested wiring to operate brake lights and car horns.

"We want youth to have some skills that put food on the table," Haba said. "We are establishing a full-fledged technical training institute, but it is very expensive. We are looking for more private sector involvement in this. We think everybody should view this as a national priority."

One of the pioneers of technical and vocational training in Rwanda is a young American woman, Elizabeth Dearborn Davis, who moved to Rwanda about six years ago after graduating from Vanderbilt University. Even after facing some initial challenges, Dearborn Davis remained undeterred in her determination to make a difference and raised new funds from individuals and family foundations worldwide. Thanks to her efforts, the Akilah Institute for Women provides business education and career development for young women. It now offers two-year business diplomas in hospitality management and entrepreneurship, with its first class graduating in August 2012. Other career tracks, including sustainable agriculture, will be added shortly.

Akilah works closely with the local private sector on curricula development and job placement. Tuition is about $3,300 per year, of which students pay $300 and Akilah raises $3,000 in scholarships. The plan is to eventually move to a sliding scale based on economic need. "Right now, the women coming into the school have a very low income, so even $300 is a lot of money. We help them to get part-time jobs," Dearborn Davis said.

The curriculum for hospitality includes front office operations, customer care, software applications, ecotourism/conservation, financial accounting, and small-business management, as well as English, leadership, and ethics. Many professionals in Rwanda's business community, including restaurateurs and hotel executives, are guest teachers at Akilah. "We have 100 percent job placement for our first graduates. Fifteen of them are going to the Marriott in Dubai for nine months before coming back here to Kigali in supervisory positions at the new Marriott that is opening here. Others are working for local hotels, tourism companies, and so forth. We are very excited for them," Dearborn Davis said.

Higher education is also a priority in Rwanda, with programs such as the Presidential Scholars, which provides a four-year scholarship to U.S. colleges and universities for Rwanda's best math and science students, who pursue engineering, computer science, and other fields so critical to Rwanda's economic development. Students receiving scholarships are expected to return to Rwanda after they have completed their education. Enrollment in public and private universities in Rwanda is also on the rise; there are currently about 60,000 university students in the country. Advanced degree offerings are expanding, including a new partnership between Carnegie Mellon University and the Rwandan government to offer a master's degree in information technology in Rwanda. Given Rwanda's dream of becoming an IT hub with a thriving ICT economy one day, the collaboration with Carnegie Mellon is a strong endorsement. The partnership intends to introduce new models of education, research and development, and commercialization of ICT.

Although encouraging university students remains a focus of Rwanda's education agenda, emphasis has shifted to basic learning, especially given the country's limited resources. "We believe someone can do without a university degree, but as a matter of basic necessity they need to read, write, and count," said Haba. "We want to support Rwandans who cannot afford higher education, but not at the expense of their younger brothers and sisters."

The Rwandan government emphasizes the importance of early childhood development by fostering the establishment of preschools. While studying education in Rwanda, American researcher Ann Kimbrough was pleased to learn that a "clergy-entrepreneur"—Rev. Dr. Laurent Mbanda, the bishop who heads the Anglican Shyira Diocese in northern Rwanda—has opened 179 preschools in a two-year period in extremely poor rural areas. (He also plans to open a university in 2014.) She cited schools as part of the solution to the ongoing challenge in Rwanda "to educate adults and children in areas relevant to their experiences and future."

At the Groupe Scolaire Kagugu school outside Kigali, students in blue and white uniforms walking across the schoolyard were distracted, as young children anywhere would be, by the unexpected presence of visitors. Suddenly, giggling students appeared at windows and doorways before being told gently but firmly that they needed to get to their classrooms. Groupe Scolaire Kagugu is a model school with an enrollment of 4,375 pupils and class sizes that average 46 students. Edouard Nizeyimana, the head teacher, described the mission of the school in words that resonated with their universality: "We want to see how we can improve the quality of education [by] having qualified teachers doing what they are supposed to do."

One of the distinguishing features of the school's instruction is the introduction of technology, even to the youngest students. It received 3,000 small, basic laptops through the One Laptop Per Child program at the end of 2008, putting technology into the hands of some of the youngest Rwandans, a key step toward realizing the country's ambition of growing an ICT economy. (Amazingly, three years after the donation, 2,954 of the tiny computers were still functioning, and most of the 46 others were awaiting repairs.)

The school also boasts a modest library, with books in English and Kinyarwanda, reflecting the drive to foster a reading culture in Rwanda, an initiative that is supported in particular by First Lady Jeannette Kagame. Indeed, having more libraries in schools to promote reading and English fluency is on Haba's wish list of initiatives.

In education, like everything else, the list of plans and goals is very long, with incremental progress that is often slow but always deliberate. "The good thing about education is it's not a drop in the ocean. Everything you do touches a life, and that life will touch another life," Haba reflected.

The third area in which Rwanda has been able to make a measurable difference at the bottom of the socioeconomic pyramid is health care, a high-touch sector that directly impacts the quality of life of all Rwandans, especially the most vulnerable. "The government decided that the country's most precious resource was its people, and therefore decided to invest in the people's health and their education," said Dr. Richard Sezibera, who served as the minister of health from October 2008 until April 2011, when he became secretary general of the East African Community. "Health in Rwanda is not only about prevention of disease, but also about contributing to the economic and social vision of the country."

In health care, Rwanda has made strides through decentralization, pushing resources such as health workers and clinics down to the local level and supporting them at the regional level. In health care, as in education and in every other sector within Rwanda, it is important to measure the current state of

achievement against the devastation during the genocide. According to a 2009 field study report, the health system had collapsed during the genocide, and more than 80 percent of the
country's health professionals were either killed or fled the country. "Post-genocide, Rwanda confronted the challenge of rebuilding the health system while simultaneously re-establishing a
social and political order based on inclusiveness, reconciliation,
and unity."[6]

Health care resources in Rwanda are scarce. The crown jewel
of its system, King Faisal Hospital in Kigali, is internationally ac-
credited, recently got its first MRI machine, and has a dialysis
unit. But specialists are rare; currently, there are no oncologists
practicing in Rwanda, although visiting physicians from other
countries help fill the gap. The need for more physicians, especially trained specialists, is an acute problem, according to Dr.
Alex Butera, an orthopedic surgeon who is also CEO of King
Faisal Hospital. Nonetheless, the presence of a medical center
like King Faisal Hospital, in a stable and secure political environment, may help transform the facility to a regional medical
center, attracting patients from across East Africa. In addition,
sufficient health care resources will help attract and maintain the
expatriate population, and therefore encourage foreign direct
investment.

Where Rwanda has truly moved the needle in terms of service delivery in health care is at the local level. Here, Rwanda has
partnered with the best: world leaders in global health and infectious diseases such as HIV/AIDS, malaria, and drug-resistant
tuberculosis. The success of the programs is in the numbers. According to a 2011 World Health Organization report, Rwanda
achieved a greater than 50 percent reduction in either confirmed

malaria cases or malaria admissions and deaths in recent years. Distribution of bed nets and mosquito spraying has reduced the incidence of malaria by some 60 percent, while health workers go house-to-house across the country to promote treatment.[7]

With HIV/AIDS, education and awareness emphasizes prevention and sexual abstinence, as well as access to antiretroviral drugs. Sezibera spoke proudly of the country's willingness to "break the taboo" to talk about HIV/AIDS in 1995 and 1996, at a time when other developing countries were downplaying the extent of the problem. The World Health Organization has cited eight countries, including Rwanda, as having achieved universal access to antiretroviral treatment for adults.

A critical factor in the development of health care has been effective partnerships between the Rwandan government and the international health community. Dr. Paul Farmer is a true pioneer in global health. Trained as a medical anthropologist and a physician, his many titles include chair of the Department of Global Health and Social Medicine at Harvard Medical School. After working around the globe, from Haiti to Peru to Russia, Farmer came to Rwanda under another professional title, as co-founder of Partners In Health.

"This is a well-run place, and that makes all the difference in public health. When you have a strong public sector with a national strategy and a commitment to delivery, that makes the work—even though it's daunting—more doable," said Farmer. "It was President Clinton who said to me while we were in Haiti in 2002 that Rwanda is a place to watch and a government to watch and a leader to watch."

Another big impetus to come to Rwanda was that Kagame and the Rwandan Ministry of Health invited Partners In Health and the Clinton Foundation to partner on health initiatives. That level of cooperation with the government is not always a given in public health projects. When Partners In Health arrived in Rwanda in the early 2000s, health care infrastructure was nearly nonexistent outside Kigali. HIV/AIDS treatment, in particular, was only accessible in the capital city. Today, Rwanda has a network of hospitals, health centers, and community-based health workers across the country.

"I would not be surprised if, in a decade, Rwanda has the strongest health system in East Africa, if not the whole continent," Farmer observed.

In 2011, Partners In Health in Rwanda served a total population of 800,000, supported three district hospitals and 37 health centers, and logged 660,137 patient visits. "Partners In Health is the largest non-governmental purveyor of health care in the country, but we work exclusively within the public sector to strengthen health systems and public institutions," said Dr. Peter Drobac, director of Partners In Health/Inshuti Mu Buzima, who lives in Rwanda. He is also an associate physician in the Division of Global Health Equity at Brigham and Women's Hospital, a teaching hospital affiliate of Harvard Medical School.

Among the many accomplishments of Partners In Health in Rwanda, in partnership with the Ministry of Health and the local community, is the construction of the state-of-the-art, 150-bed Butaro Hospital in Burera District in northern Rwanda, which was the last district in the country without a hospital. Its features include a natural ventilation system to prevent the spread of tuberculosis and courtyard gardens that entice patients outside. It also seeks to create a "center of excellence" in Rwanda to attract valuable health resources and clinical talent. In Rwanda, approximately 50 to 100 doctors graduate each year, and all are expected to provide two years of service in a rural hospital. Based on their class rank, the graduating doctors are given their preference of desired slots.

"For the last several years, the top 10 percent of the slots have gone to three rural hospitals supported by Partners In Health . . . because the quality of care there is excellent," Drobac explained. "These doctors get to interact with health professionals from around the world. Many of these cream-of-the-crop young doctors come out of Kigali for the first time and end up staying in the rural hospitals."

The health care sector has also attracted tireless champions such as Drs. Caleb and Louise King, medical missionaries who moved to Rwanda from the United States with their four children. They ended up at the Shyira Hospital in northern Rwanda, which had been devastated by the war. Slowly the hospital came back to life and became functional again, as new buildings were constructed and others were renovated. The process reflected renewal of the surrounding community. "Every year at Shyira, we saw advancement in reconciliation," Caleb King told us. His comments were yet another reminder of the interconnectedness of Rwanda's economic and social programs. When people feel their needs are being met, cohesion and community building are naturally strengthened.

Health care delivery at the grassroots in Rwanda involves workers such as midwives who are given additional training to help triage patients, as well as mobile phones that allow them to send a message to district health officials to get more information or to bring help to transport a patient to a nearby hospital. As basic as they are, the local health posts are the backbone of care delivery. Moreover, these interventions have helped reduce infant mortality to 50 per 1,000 live births in 2011 from 86 in 2006.

Universal health insurance, which is available to all Rwandans at a cost of about $2 per year, has also strengthened access to health care. Those who are too poor to afford the premium are helped by their communities. In 2010, about 92 percent of Rwandans were covered. A 2010 *New York Times* article spotlighted Rwanda's universal health coverage in contrast with the United States, which at the time was in the throes of debate over health care reform. The article quoted an editorial writer for a Rwandan newspaper who observed that Rwanda insures more of its citizens than the world's richest country.[8]

Health challenges remain, including a high birthrate, a major concern for the most densely populated country in Africa. The total fertility rate has declined, to 4.6 children per woman in 2010–2011, from 6.1 in 2006, thanks to increased use of modern contraceptives.

Another health problem being addressed, albeit slowly, is indoor pollution due to charcoal cook stoves, which causes respiratory problems in children and adults. Even casual observers notice the smell of charcoal smoke and wood fires that hangs in the air and the runny noses and coughs of some of the children. Within the Rwandan government, the Ministry of Defense is promoting what it calls an improved cook stove, which uses 75 percent less wood than traditional stoves, thus reducing smoke and related health risks, as well as environmental hazards such as deforestation.

The cook stove cause has another champion within Rwanda: a high-energy social entrepreneur named Eric Reynolds, an

American who founded the Marmot outdoor clothing and gear company that pioneered the use of the high-performance Gore-Tex fabric. Reynolds, who now lives in Rwanda, launched a new venture, Inyenyeri, to distribute a clean-burning stove that uses pellets made from ground biomass, such as fallen branches, waste vegetation, and post-harvest bean plants. (No large branches are accepted into the system, to discourage deforestation.)

The byproduct of the burning process is carbon-dense "biochar," which Reynolds calls a "soil amendment" that also helps to sequester carbon dioxide instead of releasing it into the atmosphere. The Inyenyeri business model is to give away the stoves and pellets in rural areas in return for collection of waste biomass that people bring to collection hubs for conversion into pellets. In urban areas, the pellets would be sold at a very low cost—far below that of charcoal, which produces the problematic, sooty smoke.

"We are providing a product: energy to cook, which every household in the world spends money on every day. It's that fundamental," Reynolds told us. "If we can provide that energy free to the majority of the Rwandan population that's rural and sell fuel in the city that is below the price of charcoal, and provide a stove that is cheaper—that is the hook. Nothing is more powerful of an incentive than something that is cheap or free."

How well the Inyenyeri stove project will catch on remains to be seen. What is most significant, perhaps, is the awareness that it brings to the very real needs of people at the bottom of the socioeconomic pyramid who represent the majority of the Rwandan population and the ultimate source of its stability. "One thing I like is the attitude in Rwanda, which is not about 'may do' but is about 'we will' and 'we do,'" commented

John Gara, CEO of the Rwanda Development Board. "There are things that we've done so far over the last five years, which are the foundation for what is coming next. To give you an example, we spent the past five years doing the infrastructure for ICT. What comes next is how does that impact the average person, and not just the business? How is it going to impact the health centers and the services they provide? How is it going to impact the schools? I can tell you, that is a passion of the president. When you talk to him, it's not about 'yes, business is important and investment is important.' At the end of the day, [it's the impact] on somebody in the village. Over the next five years, I expect a lot of focus on that."

The more Rwanda can address the needs of these people, the more it can advance on all fronts: not only economically, but socially and politically as well, with strides made in reconciliation and unification. As Rwanda strives to achieve its vision of a unified nation, progress must be measured at the local level. That is where people need to feel included and empowered and see the benefits of a government and a society that provide access to education, health care, and advancements in agriculture to promote a better life for all Rwandans.

8

DEVELOPING FROM WITHIN

A night flight into Kigali airport heads toward a web of light as the capital city comes into view. What is telling, though, is the vast darkness surrounding it. The view demonstrates two of Rwanda's most persistent and urgent infrastructure challenges: energy and electrification. As of the end of 2011, only 10.8 percent of households had electricity, and the current targets of a 16 percent electrification rate in 2012 and 35 percent by 2020 are ambitious. Even in Kigali, there are poor neighborhoods in which residents cannot afford an electrical connection. A recent study found only 6 percent of residents in the capital city used electricity for cooking, while 73 percent relied on it for lighting; everyone else turned to charcoal, firewood, and kerosene.

In order for Rwanda to transform itself into a middle-income country, it needs continuous infrastructure expansion, encompassing a variety of projects and priorities. It must upgrade its transportation systems, including improved roads and highways, a potential rail link to a seaport located 1,600 kilometers away, and a new international airport to expand the country's capacity to handle both passenger and cargo traffic. Rwanda's internal development needs do not end there. As the economy shifts away from subsistence agriculture, new communities must be planned to help provide affordable housing in urban and semi-urban areas.

Although diverse, such infrastructure projects have commonalities. The most obvious is that they all advance the goals set in Rwanda's Vision 2020. Paved roads and improved access to electricity are visible signs of progress and lower the cost of doing business in Rwanda. All these initiatives also depend on forming partnerships with the private sector and attracting foreign direct investment. Given the price tags of large infrastructure projects—hundreds of millions of dollars—the Rwandan government must engage investors and strategic partners who will need to earn a return in order to commit the necessary money and technical expertise. Megadeals in infrastructure may challenge the human resource capacity of some government ministries and agencies, particularly at the middle and lower levels. At the top, however, there are eager and informed individuals pushing toward execution in alignment with the priorities set by President Paul Kagame. Therefore, as more infrastructure deals are put in place, Rwanda's emerging leaders will learn by doing, gaining competence and confidence, and establishing a proven track record of success.

Of Rwanda's infrastructure needs, clearly the most urgent is energy. In 2000, when its Vision 2020 was adopted, 99 percent of the population used wood for energy, which led to massive deforestation and soil erosion. At the time, petroleum product imports consumed more than 40 percent of Rwanda's foreign exchange. Today, energy remains the top priority for Rwanda's development and attainment of its Vision 2020 goals.

"Energy is a major impediment. How do we produce enough? How do we make it accessible to as many Rwandans as possible, because there is very little you can do without accessible energy," commented Foreign Minister Louise Mushikiwabo.

"Energy is the starting point," added Minister of Infrastructure Albert Nsengiyumva. "It is needed in every other sector."

The current available electrical generating capacity is estimated at about 80 to 100 megawatts, while the country's eventual needs are pegged at 1,000 megawatts. Although the challenge is significant, considering where the country was less than two decades ago, progress has been impressive. "If you looked at Rwanda in 1994 compared to now, you can see how much electricity there is—not just generation, but also distribution to send it to as many remote areas as possible," explained John Gara, CEO of the Rwanda Development Board. "In 1994, if you flew over the country it was all dark, even Kigali. So certainly electrification is going to have an impact; it already has."

To improve distribution of electricity, Rwanda is exploring a variety of generation projects that will increase the capacity of its national grid and provide on-site power in isolated rural areas. When it comes to energy, strategic investments from foreign entities with financial, human capital, and technology resources are crucial. "It's the financial resources first; we need money," Nsengiyumva said. "Producing electricity is very costly. A hydroelectric dam that can produce up to 28 megawatts [of electricity] can cost up to $100 million to develop . . . so we have to mobilize resources."

One of Rwanda's new energy projects has a high international profile largely because of the technology involved. The KivuWatt project developed by ContourGlobal, a New York–based international power company, will extract and process methane gas dissolved in the waters of Lake Kivu, a 1,500-foot-deep body of water in western Rwanda, to power 100 megawatts of electricity generating capacity. The gas reserves in the lake are huge, estimated at 60 billion cubic meters. ContourGlobal will not be the first to harness lake gas for production of electricity, but far smaller plants have seen limited success, primarily because of the difficulty of isolating methane from dissolved lake water. Perhaps the most useful analogy is bubbles in champagne. In the case of champagne, the gas in the liquid is carbon dioxide, a by-product of fermentation. The waters of Lake Kivu contain pockets of methane, which can be volatile, as well as carbon dioxide and other potentially harmful gases. Therefore, safe extraction of the gas would not only produce electricity, but could also reduce health and safety hazards by lowering the risk of a catastrophic release of gases trapped in Lake Kivu, which is surrounded by more than 2 million inhabitants. (In 1986, 1,700 people in the valley below Lake Nyos in Cameroon died when carbon dioxide gas bubbled out of the lake and asphyxiated them.[1])

ContourGlobal has developed what it believes to be a unique separation process that will be housed, together with other processing equipment, on a gas extraction barge moored 13 kilometers offshore. This gas extraction facility, roughly 70 meters by 30 meters, will raise the gas from a depth of 350 meters, process it, and then send it by pipeline to an onshore generating facility. From there, transformers and transmission lines connect the electricity generated by the plant to Rwanda's national grid, all of which is scheduled to start in late 2012.

Phase One of ContourGlobal's plan calls for 25 megawatts of power generation. This will be followed by an assessment of the project's effect on the methane resource as well as the biodiversity of the lake, which is used extensively for fishing. After the impact study is concluded, the project will be scaled to 100 megawatts. "Given where Rwanda's electricity generation capacity is now, adding 100 megawatts to it will be huge," said Richard Wilcock, senior vice president of engineering services for ContourGlobal. Still, the country needs so much more, revealing the potential for other projects to be developed. (ContourGlobal, for example, is also proposing a separate solar power generation project for Rwanda.)

The KivuWatt project won the 2011 Africa Power Deal of the Year from Euromoney's *Project Finance* magazine, a third such honor for ContourGlobal, which has 2,370 megawatts of installed capacity in operation or under construction in 14 countries. Agreements for KivuWatt's $91.25 million financing were signed in August 2011, with a lending group that includes the Emerging Africa Infrastructure Fund, Netherlands Development Finance Company (FMO), the African Development Bank, and the Belgian Investment Company for Developing Countries. The balance of the $142 million project cost was provided by ContourGlobal.

"The opportunity to take part in a project that provides so much benefit in a postconflict environment, including providing electricity critical to Rwanda's continued economic growth—and at the same time reducing the risk of a catastrophic release of the lake gases—was very attractive to our lending group,"

William Barry, vice president of business development for ContourGlobal and the KivuWatt project manager, told us. "The
ones that we signed with were the ones who were willing to
accept and share the risks of such a novel technology, and in
such a remote location." Indeed, in an announcement about the
Deal of the Year award, lenders added their glowing statements
about the project: "The [African Development Bank] is proud
to support this project, which is an example of how to adapt an
advanced technology to a unique country situation: the methane
which lies beneath Lake Kivu will be converted into critical electricity for Rwandans, while reducing greenhouse gas emissions,"
stated Tim Turner, director of private sector operations for the
development bank.[2]

ContourGlobal first became interested in the Lake Kivu
project when CEO Joseph Brandt visited Rwanda in 2007. Since
then, the story of the project has been one of patience and of
procuring the necessary permits and agreements, but also of cooperation among the Ministries of Energy, Infrastructure, and
Finance, as well as the Rwanda Development Board. By early
2012, they had signed the concession for 100 megawatts, financing was in place, and the equipment for the power plant and gas
extraction facility was being delivered to the remote site from
more than a dozen different countries.

With every investment, Rwanda seeks opportunities for
training and employment for its people. ContourGlobal will initially hire a combination of expatriates and Rwandans as operators, and is partnering with the African Development Bank
to build a technical center to train Rwandans to work on the
KivuWatt project and, longer term, to take over operations after
the 25-year concession agreement expires.

To meet its electricity needs and reduce reliance on expensive foreign petroleum product imports, Rwanda is also exploring other energy sources, including geothermal. The presence of hot springs and steam underground has given the country hopes of exploiting this renewable resource and attracting investors. "Geothermal is very critical, and it is also renewable," Nsengiyumva said. "The initial feasibility study suggests that we have good capacity."

One of the first sites to be tested is at Karisimbi, a dormant volcano in the Virunga Mountain Range in northern Rwanda, an area of seismic activity. If exploratory drilling and testing of three wells prove productive, a 10-megawatt, steam-driven electrical plant will be built there. The government is also evaluating two other geothermal sites (Kinigi and Gisenyi) in western Rwanda and one in the southwestern region (Bugarama). The region in the west, however, is the most advanced. Geoscientific studies have already been carried out there, and the plan is eventually to develop four power plants in that region, each with the capacity to generate 75 megawatts of power, which together would add 300 megawatts to Rwanda's power grid by 2017. (The timeline will depend on the success of exploration as well as private sector interest in development.) Initial surveys reveal the potential eventually to generate 740 megawatts from geothermal energy. The Japan International Cooperation Agency has provided experts in geothermal exploration and has pledged to provide technical support as the projects continue. Other potential development and financial partners include Belgian Technical Cooperation, a Belgian development agency; France's development agency, and the European Investment Bank.

In addition, Rwanda is exploring hydropower development, including microprojects that produce a relatively small amount of energy, but can provide power to a community or even a hospital. For example, the United Nations Industrial Development Organization has a partnership with the Rwandan government to develop small-scale hydroelectric plants, particularly in rural areas that are too expensive to connect to the national power grid.

CONNECTING A LANDLOCKED COUNTRY

Rwanda's need for connections extends beyond its power grid. The country's second-biggest infrastructure need is transportation. In a landlocked country, with the nearest port about 1,600 kilometers away, ground transportation remains very expensive. Roads and highways are improving all over the country, though, both around Kigali and in rural areas. Here, public-private partnerships have created opportunities for both investment and job creation. Horizon Group, a Rwandan investment fund that invests military pensions, has established a construction company to break into road construction, which previously had been dominated by Chinese and European contractors. Horizon Construction started with smaller projects, roads that were only two- to five-kilometers long.

With a mission to incubate local participation in key economic sectors, Horizon saw the opportunity to move into highway construction and to develop skills among Rwandans. When other local contractors emerge, Horizon will move on to other businesses—for example, constructing hydroelectric power plants. "We are trying to create as many private sector companies as we can by looking for opportunities where we lack private sector capacity," said Horizon Group CEO Eugene Haguma. "It's not just about any opportunity. If something is not being done, then we have to address it."

Within the transportation sector, there is another crucial project that, if it materializes, could significantly reduce the cost of Rwandan imports and exports. A proposed rail link that would connect Rwanda and Burundi with the port of Dar es Salaam in Tanzania has been in the planning stage for the past several years. The project, with a reported price tag of about $5 billion, has been targeted as a priority investment for the East African Community. At 1,670 kilometers, which would make it the longest in the region, the rail line would require cooperation among three neighboring countries: Rwanda, Burundi, and Tanzania. As of mid-2012, a detailed technical study was being undertaken by Canadian consulting firm Canarail, and a full environmental study was also underway. Cost estimates will be refined based upon the findings of the engineering study. Final results are expected in early 2013.

Further along is the proposal to build a new airport, which would allow greater use of regional air transport for goods as well as passengers. "If we want to position Rwanda as attractive for investors and for tourism, the airport plays an important part," Nsengiyumva said. The CAPA Centre for Aviation called Rwanda's proposed new Bugesera International Airport, to be located about 25 kilometers outside Kigali, "perhaps the most notable event" in African aviation. The Rwandan government has advertised for bids to design, build, finance, maintain, and operate the airport, which is expected to be completed in 2016 at an estimated cost of several hundred million dollars. (Early estimates reportedly swelled from about $300 million to $600 million, but have since been scaled back.) It received 37 applications, of which they identified 11 potential candidates.[3]

Given the scope and timeline of the new airport project, the Rwandan government is moving ahead with a more immediate investment, reportedly committing $17 million to upgrade the existing Kigali International Airport. Three years ago, traffic in the airport amounted to 100 to 150 passengers per hour during peak hours; now that number is up to 500 passengers. Further, increases in cargo flights have raised air traffic at the airport, now amounting to 200 scheduled flights per week, up from 40 to 60 flights per week 2 years ago.[4] As arriving passengers who have crowded six deep around two overloaded baggage conveyors during peak hours could attest, Kigali airport is in need of newer and expanded facilities. The plan includes new luggage belts and check-in areas, as well as amenities like duty-free shops, business lounges, and restaurants.

In discussions about Rwanda's high-price infrastructure projects, from airports to a rail line to power plants, we heard questions about the quality of the advice available to the government. Getting a variety of opinions and, more to the point, listening to the most informed sources will be crucial to making solid judgment calls, particularly with hundreds of millions of dollars at stake. One rich resource is the Presidential Advisory Council, comprised of Rwandans and foreigners with varied expertise and backgrounds, from business to academics. In addition, there is borrowed talent from abroad who give of their time, talent, and expertise, as well as Rwandans who have returned to their country after living and working in Europe and/or the United States. Crucial to these relationships is an honest and open flow of information, including about obstacles and set-backs. For Kagame and his ministers, planning and executing large-scale projects must be accompanied by robust fact-finding and consultation with experts in order to gather as many per-spectives as possible.

In addition to energy and transportation, a third infrastruc-ture priority in Rwanda is housing. Kigali has a variety of hous-ing stock, from modern homes to far more modest structures of mud bricks with no running water or indoor plumbing. One so-lution they are actively exploring, especially in Kigali, is planned communities. Although for us that phrase might conjure images of gated grounds in Florida with a recreation center and a nine-hole golf course, in Kigali the concept is based on the *umudu-gudu* neighborhood: bringing people together with access to the necessary infrastructure such as streets, electricity, and water.

One company that has its eyes on such development is Re-naissance Partners, which is part of the investment firm Renais-sance Group that specializes in emerging markets. Renaissance Partners is involved in private equity development in real estate, focusing on peri-urban renewal, meaning developments at or near the city limits. Renaissance is among the firms that devel-oped Tatu City, a mixed-use planned community outside Nai-robi, Kenya, which was designed to house 62,000 residents and several businesses on a 1,000-hectare (2,400 acre) site. Now, Re-naissance Partners is working with the Rwandan government to develop a large tract of land outside Kigali, for which it would play the role of master developer.

Kigali, which has a population of about one million, is ex-pected to reach two million over the next ten years, making it a suitable site for urban planned communities. Within Kigali there is huge residential demand but limited mortgage capacity; to meet the needs for housing and financing, a lender will be brought in to provide mortgage financing to consumers. "It's a very important target market for us," said Graeme Reid of Renaissance Partners. "The model we follow is based on rapid urbanization and rapid economic growth that creates a middle class."

Another entrant in the housing market is Horizon Group, which hopes to develop its "Horizon Villages" model to address the social, education, and business needs of residents in a community. "We are trying as much as possible to reduce their dependence on the land," Haguma said. Development of these communities also allows people to migrate out of rural areas and off land that can be used for agriculture. Within the planned communities, small businesses and services would provide employment opportunities.

Horizon Group has bought 30 hectares (72 acres) of land in the city with plans to develop its first model village. "We don't want to push people into living the way we think is the right way," Haguma added. "It's creating a neighborhood to attract people."

ATTRACTING INVESTORS

With such ambitious plans, Rwanda has had to add another type of capacity—this time of the institutional variety, through the Rwanda Development Board, known by everyone as the RDB. In the quiet offices of the RDB, there is intensity and focus. Clare Akamanzi, chief operating officer, tapped a note to a colleague on her electronic PDA to check on the status of a pending matter involving a Western enterprise. "We'll get an answer in a day or two," Akamanzi promised. Within an hour, she did.

One of the top priorities for the RDB is soliciting investors for development projects, particularly in infrastructure. When we talked with Akamanzi, her team had just come back from Turkey and was leaving in a week's time for India and China.

Rwanda has also made great strides in opening doors for business, particularly among its local entrepreneurs. The World Bank's "Doing Business Report 2012" ranked Rwanda in forty-fifth place worldwide for ease of doing business, up from fiftieth place in 2011, thanks to reforms enacted by the government to attract business, promote entrepreneurship, and grow the private sector. Rwanda stands as the second-most-reformed country in terms of doing business over the five-year period from 2006 to 2011, behind the Republic of Georgia. With a "one-stop center" to complete registration forms, RDB makes it possible for a would-be entrepreneur to incorporate a business within 24 hours.

John Gara, CEO of the RDB, credited reforms for improving efficiency and streamlining processes, such as the repeal of laws that created unnecessary bureaucracy. "There is a tendency anywhere in the world, when people are used to doing things a certain way, for there to be reluctance to get rid of bureaucracy. For some of those in government, bureaucracy is something that they enjoy. It gives them more work. The more papers there are to stamp and sign, the more reason they have to be there," he added. "When you start removing some of the bureaucratic things in government, there is resistance because you are changing how things have always been done. But you find that it actually works better. . . . People didn't need to file five papers; one is enough and [the process] still works."

The RDB, which is based on the Singapore Economic Development Board, is the go-to destination for virtually all deals and investment. Ideally, it promotes efficiency and coordination so investors do not have to run from ministry to ministry trying to get documents signed and approvals finalized. In talking with investors and business people alike, we heard some mixed reviews for the RDB. Many people spoke highly of the institution and in particular its top management. Others complained about delays as processes became bogged down in bureaucracy at lower levels at RDB and government ministries. Although Rwanda boasts zero tolerance for corruption, which is a very significant selling point for attracting investors, excessive bureaucracy can be nearly as counterproductive.

Refreshingly, Gara spoke candidly about those frustrations and pledged improvements in responsiveness and customer service attitudes. He acknowledged that there have been problems for established businesses, which need support to resolve issues that arise. Gara shared a story about receiving a text message on his phone complaining about the business registration department at the RDB. He immediately sent a text back, asking for more details, including the person's name. The person replied, "I'm just a Rwandan who is not feeling very good about what is happening." Gara went downstairs to business registration and called the phone number on the text message. The man who answered was surprised that the head of the RDB was on the phone, wanting to know about his problems and how he could help. The story had a happy ending, but it pointed to a bigger problem within RDB and other institutions of government:

dealing with delays caused by a lack of human capital capacity in terms of know-how, execution, and follow through. These issues become more acute with larger, complicated deals.

Increasingly, Gara pledged, the RDB will take on an advocacy role for investors who find the process has suddenly become bogged down. "For example, if an investor buys land to put up the hotel and has the money and everything, but now wants a construction permit and it's taking forever, that is where we need to come in. The RDB will do its best to help," he added.

Advocacy, however, does not mean the RDB will automatically grant every investor's wish. "If someone says to us, 'I want a fifteen-year tax holiday,' and that 'these other countries give a tax holiday, so why don't you,' I am happy to say, 'In Rwanda, we don't,'" Gara clarified.

Most big-name investors, however, are reasonable in their requests and not seeking unfair advantage, Gara noted. However, there is an attitude among some in government, especially those who are inexperienced in dealing with foreign investors, that these business arrangements are somehow exploitative and, therefore, not in Rwanda's best interest. "Some people think that if a foreign investor starts making a lot of profit, he's exploiting. It's not exploiting; he's doing a very good business. It's helping to grow the economy," Gara added.

In order for Rwanda to move forward with infrastructure development, private sector involvement and foreign investment are crucial. The government simply does not have the resources, financial or technological, to tackle the large-scale projects that will move the country toward its goals. Partnerships are the only way forward, with the government granting concessions and opening business opportunities in order to attract investors.

Although the process can be daunting for all parties, there is great progress to report. Deals are being signed and infrastructure is being developed, from highways to power plants.

Most important is the will to succeed, backed by a firm but positive tone set by the president and echoed through the ministries and into the private sector. As Haguma of Horizon Group told us, "When leadership has confidence, people are told, 'You can do this.'" In Rwanda, despite gaps in expertise and bureaucratic delays at times, there is no shortage of can-do attitude. In a country that is both a work *in* progress and a work *of* progress, the wheels continue to turn. Given the magnitude of its needs, odds favor more progress, which will light up Rwandan skies—literally.

9

OPENING THE DOOR
TO FOREIGN DIRECT
INVESTMENT

The world was literally open to Visa Inc. as it looked at where to launch innovative electronic payments and banking products for consumers in developing economies. As it narrowed its focus on sub-Saharan Africa, six finalist countries emerged, among them Rwanda. Meetings with the central bank and several financial institutions helped Visa gain deeper insights into the needs of Rwandan consumers, which include many who are "unbanked," but have mobile telephones that can be used for things like making payments or transferring cash. The real selling point, however, was the Rwandan government itself; it simply wanted Visa more palpably than any of the other candidates.

"The government is the number one reason why we're in Rwanda: its forward-thinking and strategic agenda, the way it's focused on ICT [information and communications technology] development, and its very pro-private sector-led development," said Ginger Baker, an American business development executive for Visa who moved to Kigali with her husband and young son in 2011. "Rwanda was eager for our investment."

In late December 2011, Visa and the government of Rwanda announced a collaboration agreement to build electronic payment infrastructure in the country, begin local processing of payments and settlement services, and develop training programs for Rwandans. Installing the Rwanda Integrated Payments Processing System will help the country transition to cashless and electronic commerce products. Then, as Visa expands its mobile banking and e-commerce solutions throughout the region, the payment processing system will likely see increased volume, which will help Rwanda in its pursuit of becoming an ICT hub.

Visa's services extend to all levels of the socioeconomic pyramid. At the top, more ATMs are being installed in the country to dispense cash to consumers with Visa cards, a service that will also appeal to tourists and business visitors. Visa's advertising, which is highly visible throughout Kigali, conspicuously displays a 5,000 Rwandan franc bill (equivalent to about $8) instead of Visa's usual graphic of an American $20 bill. And although the ATM service is important, the focus of the Visa venture is not cash; rather, it is cashless. Visa works with almost all of the banks in Rwanda, and is rolling out financial products including credit and prepaid debit cards, initially through Bank of Kigali, Equity Bank, and Ecobank, a Togo-based pan-African bank. In addition, Visa is also working with RwandAir, the national air carrier, to develop online ticketing and reservation services. Ambassador Claver Gatete, governor of the National Bank of Rwanda, has hailed the Visa partnership as a way to reduce the widespread use of cash and increase liquidity in the banking system, which helps to reduce interest rates and improve price stability.

In addition, Visa is reaching out to people who previously had little or no access to financial services with new solutions such as mobile banking via cell phone. Admittedly, women making $2 a day would not be the typical Visa clientele. In Rwanda, however, they are the customers of microfinance banks like Urwego Opportunity Bank, one of the first institutions to partner with Visa and its subsidiary, Fundamo, to launch banking products on mobile phones in Rwanda. These consumers are especially interested in cash transfers, which typically happen within a community or among extended family members. To educate these consumers, Visa has rolled out a financial literacy project that includes lessons on budgeting, saving, and making payments.

Visa's announcement made news not only in Rwanda but across the international financial press. The *Wall Street Journal* noted, "The agreement aims to get Visa's cards into the hands of average Rwandans, many of whom don't have bank accounts. The pact will also help test appetite in the last largely untapped financial services markets in the world: Africa."[1]

The Visa partnership, like all new developments in Rwanda, is even more noteworthy when viewed through the lens of where the country has been. During the genocide, commerce and banking collapsed, as did incomes. The ruling regime pilfered the treasury, leaving the national coffers empty. Many banks were insolvent into the early 2000s. Only by 2004 was the sector better capitalized and strengthened with a regulatory framework. "Before the financial sector could make any positive impact or any positive contribution to the economy, it had to be vibrant," said Consolate Rusagara, a former deputy governor of the Central Bank of Rwanda who is now senior adviser, Financial & Private Sector Vice Presidency, at the World Bank. Today, a marquee name like Visa greatly helps Rwanda on its quest to attract more foreign direct investment. Simply stated, Rwanda needs more companies to set up shop there if it hopes to grow the economy, create jobs, improve training and education for a skilled workforce, and expand the middle class. Foreign direct investment is an infusion not only of capital, but also of know-how—essential to incubate new businesses and industries and improve a country's global competitiveness. And success breeds success. As former investment banking executive and founder of Bridge2Rwanda and ISOKO Institute Dale Dawson observed, in Rwanda and on the African continent as a whole more foreign direct investment is needed to create and sustain a cycle of prosperity in which foreign investment fuels more wealth and wealth fuels more foreign investment.

Rwanda has laid several important foundations for foreign investment, from the fiber optic network that spans the country to its solid credit ratings and political stability. In late 2011, Standard & Poor's announced an initial "B" long-term and short-term credit rating for Rwanda with a positive outlook, citing the country's good economic performance over the last decade, decisive market-oriented reforms, good macroeconomic management, and the government's Vision 2020 plan to transform the country into a service-based middle-income country. "It has invested significantly in infrastructure and skills development and has made continuous reforms to improve the business climate," S&P stated.[2] Fitch Ratings has also given Rwanda a credit rating of "B," which acknowledges that although the country is dependent on foreign aid for 40 percent of its budget, it aims to achieve eventual economic independence through development of a services industry and an ICT-based economy.[3]

One of the earliest missions of the Rwanda Development Board has been courting investors to come explore business and investment opportunities. "The huge focus for the next few years is attracting more investment, particularly foreign investment. In my view we have not attracted as much as we'd like," said the board's CEO, John Gara. "It is our intention to target firms with international names. We've got some ICT [companies] on our list." Although he declined to give any names of possible candidates, he acknowledged there are a number of areas of ICT where Rwanda would like to focus, such as cloud computing and business process outsourcing. "We want to get some names that will make others says, 'Wait a minute. There must be something interesting about Rwanda,'" Gara added.

Some of the most visible examples of foreign direct investment to date are in the tourism sector. The Serena Hotels in Kigali and Lake Kivu are owned by the Aga Khan Fund for Economic Development. Radisson is contracted to operate a hotel and convention center currently under construction. The newest property slated to open is the Kigali Marriott, built by a consortium of Chinese and Hong Kong investors in partnership with Rwandan businessman Hatari Sekoko. "I personally brought Marriott here [to be the hotel operator]," he told us with a broad smile.

Dubbed a "king of Kigali" by *Forbes Africa,* Hatari, as everyone calls him, is an example of Rwandan entrepreneurship. Hatari started life as a refugee "born on the way out of

Rwanda," was raised in Uganda and then Kenya, and later attended college in Uganda. His first job was driving a truck, transporting goods from the Kenyan port of Mombasa; he later ferried maize day and night for USAID, which brought food supplies to Kenya during a severe drought in the 1980s. A Japanese tourist he met by chance on the beach in Kenya introduced Hatari to the business of shipping secondhand cars to markets such as New Zealand, Bangladesh, and, later, Kenya. His business career was interrupted when the Rwandan civil war broke out and he joined the Rwandan Patriotic Front (RPF). After the struggle, although he had already been discharged, he sought permission from then Vice President and Minister of Defense Paul Kagame to leave the military; as he saw it, he would be of more use to the country as a civilian businessman. After their meeting, Kagame wrote a note to Hatari's commanding officer, giving his blessing for Hatari's departure, stating, "This gentleman will be more useful leaving active service."

Listening to Hatari tell his story, business ventures quickly become *adventures*. He sobered, though, when he spoke about the opportunities he has been given, not only as an investor and businessman, but as a Rwandan who survived the civil war and genocide when so many others did not. "You have to use your time correctly and profitably, because others deserved it more than you," Hatari said.

Today, Hatari is executive director of Doyelcy Ltd., founded in 2006, one of the largest firms in Rwanda, with core businesses in hospitality, property, insurance, renewable energy, and agriculture. His landmark is the Kigali City Tower, the tallest building in Rwanda and, as *Forbes Africa* noted, "a potent symbol of reconstruction less than two decades after dead bodies littered the streets."[4] Hatari himself is an example of the new Rwanda, a hometown entrepreneur who can be a role model for the next generation of educated Rwandans. Although homegrown entrepreneurship is thus far modest in scale, Hatari shows that bigger dreams and broader plans are possible. The next generation of educated Rwandans cannot rely on the government to provide jobs for them, Hatari reminded us. Job creation will come out of the private sector and through foreign investment. (Investments from foreign and local sources totaling $626 million in 2011 are expected to generate about 9,060 new jobs, according to Rwanda Development Board statistics.[5])

THE COFFEE TEST CASE

One of the best examples of foreign direct investment is Rwanda Trading Company, a coffee exporting operation that serves several purposes: providing a test case for the government on how foreign business interests are encouraged or discouraged; expanding the sales of Rwandan coffee overseas; and making a profit. Founder Scott Ford offered this disclaimer: "I'm not a save-the-world guy." But after visiting Rwanda and then joining the Presidential Advisory Council, it became obvious to him that what the country needed was a "demonstrable example of action" to show how business could improve the lives of others. "I said, 'I don't care if it's 100 people, we have to have demonstrable examples,'" Ford recalled. "I'm all about Vision 2020, but I've been around long enough to know that we had better hit vision 2009, 2010, 2011, and so forth to get there. So I started looking for a business where the capital that I had and whatever management experience I had could have a leveraged impact."

The result was Rwanda Trading Company. Since 2009, Rwanda Trading has increased its purchases of a value-added coffee product known as fully washed beans, which are carefully processed to highlight positive flavors in Rwandan coffee. To encourage the move from semi-washed to fully washed coffee, the Rwandan government and the private sector have pushed for the establishment of additional coffee washing stations, which now number about 240 in the country.

Once the washed coffee beans arrive at Rwanda Trading operations on the outskirts of Kigali, they are sorted for color, quality, and defects by machine; premium beans are sorted by hand. Women seated on both sides of two long tables sifted their hands through green, unroasted coffee beans. A handful of beans with defects such as brown spots or irregular shape were separated. The rest were sent off to be bagged and shipped out in containers. Coffee is exported "green" and roasted near its end markets to preserve quality and taste.

In Rwanda Trading Company's coffee laboratory, a Rwandan woman who has been trained as a "cupper," a kind of in-house sommelier of coffee, evaluated brewed batches for unique flavors that might appeal to roasters. The more distinct the flavors, the better the chance upscale coffee roasters will pay a premium for the producer's beans. Already Rwandan coffee is creating a buzz. A blog for Starbucks, which sells a fair-trade Rwandan coffee called Gakenke, named for a highland district in the Northern Province, noted that Rwandan coffees "often highlight a lemony acidity, with notes of red or dark fruit and sometimes chocolate."[6]

Such attention is only possible with a higher-quality, value-added product, which for Ford means working closely with farmers, aggregators, and washing station operators to share best practices. "The next thing we have to solve is the on-the-ground impact," Ford acknowledged. "If we really want to grow the business, if we really want to be successful, we have to get good at it."

Although Ford is motivated by intrinsic reasons, including being a faith-based businessman, it is very important that Rwanda Trading Company be profitable. (The Rwandan operations were breakeven to slightly profitable for the first time in 2011, the third year of operation.) The return on investment is important because Rwanda Trading has willingly acted as a test case to help the Rwandan government discover how to improve the business climate, particularly for foreign investors. "We put on one hat when we're in the market buying coffee from the farmers. And then we put on the other hat and say to the government, 'Now we're going to give you honest feedback on the impact that your policies and regulations are having on business. This is what I think helps you and this is what hurts you.' This is the role we play," Ford explained. "The government is so open to it. They want the whole truth and nothing but the truth. They not only appreciate it, they will go and do something about it."

These lessons are important to fostering more foreign direct investment. As noted previously, a primary need throughout the public and private sector is development of human capital. Customer service skills must be elevated within sectors such as hospitality and tourism, as well as in government ministries and agencies. In addition, Rwandans must adapt more of an entrepreneurial mindset, which "was not developed here like in some East African countries such as Uganda and Kenya," said Faustin Mbundu, chairman of the Private Sector Federation.

Fortunately, there is a real thirst for knowledge and training among many young professionals. For example, a five-day financial analyst training course by Training The Street, which provides training to Wall Street firms, was oversubscribed, with 70 participants of varying degrees of skills and proficiency in subjects like financial modeling. "The desire and ambition to learn was everything we asked for," commented Alex Lue, a New York City–based trainer who was among the instructors in the Kigali program, which was a first for the country and Training The Street's second time in Africa.

Among the other lessons is better regard for "sanctity of contract," meaning the terms agreed to must be obeyed by all parties. In Rwanda, as in many foreign cultures, some view a contract and its terms—payment, delivery, and other contractual promises—as subject to reconsideration. Tom Allen, an attorney and country director for Bridge2Rwanda, offered an example in an article in *The Daedalus Experiment,* a newsletter published by Michael Fairbanks of The SEVEN Fund. Allen described a social entrepreneur who wanted to set up a food processing plant that would produce a special product for malnourished infants. A site was chosen, and the entrepreneur signed a lease agreement with an option to purchase the real property for $450,000. But after the entrepreneur finalized a business plan and secured financing, when he tried to exercise his contractual right to purchase the land for $450,000, the owner refused, and demanded $600,000. An independent appraisal determined the property was worth somewhere between $280,000 and $460,000. Although the entrepreneur took the case to court and received a judgment in his favor, he decided instead to build the facility elsewhere in Africa. "The sanctity and efficient enforceability of contract is the real lingua franca as well as the rule of the game that Rwanda wants to win," Allen wrote. "These principles should be passionately promoted by the Office of the President, the Ministry of Justice, throughout the entire government of Rwanda, all the way down to the primary schools and the churches. It should become a key component of Rwanda's greatest asset, namely, its cultural capital."[7]

Rod Reynolds, on sabbatical from his role as CEO of Scotiabank Europe Plc and a member of Kagame's Presidential Advisory Council, also cited a "lack of jurisprudence in contract law or in the rule of contracts" as one of the obstacles that could impede foreign direct investment, particularly in greenfield operations (meaning investment in land and infrastructure for a new business). Other obstacles, along with human capital issues and delays in decision making, are "obfuscated tax and VAT [value added tax] policies" and a shortage of general managers. Although such challenges might be overcome if an investment involved a country's natural resources or the acquisition of an existing company, they could prove to be prohibitive for a greenfield venture that is riskier, making investors "much more circumspect," Reynolds said in an interview with ISOKO Institute, a Kigali-based think tank.[8]

Although sobering, awareness of these obstacles allows them to be addressed, provided they are brought to peoples' attention at the highest level of government. The government's attitude on such matters appears to be one of relying on the institutions and processes that have been put in place, such as the courts. However, it may fall to the country's leaders—including Kagame, who has spoken out in the past on the need to improve customer service—to promote sanctity of contract within Rwanda. This is where the Rwandan government can truly demonstrate its strong pro-business attitude.

The Rwandan government is no stranger to business ventures. It has a track record in establishing businesses, going back to the days immediately following the genocide when the RPF utilized the "war chest" it had raised for munitions and supplies to begin providing the most basic necessities in Kigali. Kagame recalled for us how the RPF bought basic supplies such as paraffin and kerosene for lamps, salt, soap, sugar, and other basic goods in Uganda, Kenya, and Burundi to restock store shelves in Kigali and give a semblance of normalcy amid utter devastation and complete disruption. From there, the government and the RPF, sometimes separately and sometimes as partners, have been involved in a number of businesses, from bottled water to telecommunications.

Although some economists might complain that Rwanda has undermined its pro-private sector stance with heavy government involvement in businesses, other observers argue the opposite: the Rwandan government has launched businesses when no one else would, thus attracting other investors. Although there is some impatience on Kagame's part in not waiting for the private sector to act, the demonstrated willingness by the government to sell its holdings when there is private sector interest is an invaluable asset in a developing economy. For example, in October 2011, the Rwandan government and the RPF's investment arm Crystal Ventures collectively sold a 25 percent stake in MTN Rwandacell Ltd. to MTN Group of South Africa. After the transaction, MTN owns 80 percent of the Rwandan cellular business, while Crystal Ventures holds 20 percent. In a statement, Rwanda called MTN Rwandacell an "excellent investment" for the government that allowed telecommunications in the country to grow and develop: "Government has for some time now indicated its desire to no longer participate in the sector as an investor."[9]

Crystal Ventures CEO John Bosco Birungi is a Ugandan-born Rwandan who, after graduating from college in Uganda, went to the United States, where he lived from 2000 to 2008. With a dream to work on Wall Street, he started first in Boston with what was then Fleet Financial and later joined a boutique mergers and acquisitions firm while getting his MBA in finance from Brandeis University. Later, he worked on Wall Street for Bank of America in its securities division. Attracted by the business possibilities in Uganda and Rwanda, he and his partners formed an investment advisory company to promote investment opportunities in East Africa. After a chance meeting with Kagame, however, Birungi found himself recruited to be the CEO of Crystal Ventures, which seeks investment opportunities that offer a long-term return on investment while also delivering social value. Today it owns businesses in concrete, construction/civil engineering, property development, security, media, and advertising. It started a chain of Bourbon Coffee shops that feature Rwandan coffee in Washington, DC; New York; Cambridge, Mass.; and Kigali. Seven of Crystal Ventures' businesses are owned 100 percent; three are owned jointly with Rwandan partners who are individual investors.

Birungi countered the perception that Crystal Ventures, as an RPF investment company, has enjoyed an unfair advantage. "The days of monopoly for Crystal Ventures are long gone," he commented. For example, when Intersec was formed, it was the only private security company; now there are 12 competitors.

Crystal Ventures is now looking at the next step for Intersec, such as branching out into secure money transit for banks and businesses. "We take the risk, start the business, and as the sector grows and the country grows, we exit," Birungi explained. The investment horizon could range from as few as 5 to as many as 15 or even 20 years. Exit plans may include selling to a partner or other investors, or selling shares through initial public offerings (IPOs) on the new Rwanda Stock Exchange.

The Rwanda Stock Exchange may be small, but its plans are oversized. Visiting the trading floor in early 2012, we found a quiet start to a three-hour trading session, in which a handful of brokers in red jackets quietly announced their bids and offers for four stocks traded on the exchange, including the first two Rwandan IPOs, as well as a handful of Rwandan treasury bonds. The first stock on the exchange was Bralirwa, the brewery officially known as Brasseries et Limonaderies du Rwanda, which went public in January 31, 2011, as the government of Rwanda divested a 25 percent stake to the public. The government's remaining 5 percent interest was sold to majority stakeholder Heineken. The Bralirwa IPO was oversubscribed by 174 percent, indicating how much buyer interest exceeded the number of shares offered. The success of the IPO provided a boost for the Rwanda Stock Exchange, which was officially launched with the Bralirwa IPO. Since then a second Rwandan company, Bank of Kigali, has gone public. In addition, the exchange crosslists two East African companies: Kenya Commercial Bank and National Media Group of Kenya, which first traded on the Nairobi Stock Exchange.

The Rwanda Stock Exchange has allowed the country's diaspora to participate in the country's economic development. The government also plans to tap that resource by offering a "diaspora bond" to raise money to finance infrastructure development by borrowing from diaspora Rwandans, who will become bondholders.

Robert Mathu, executive director of Rwanda's Capital Market Authority, worked in the financial sector across East Africa before being hired to run Rwanda's nascent stock exchange. Although four stocks and a few bond issues hardly constitutes a big board, Mathu sees rich possibilities as more companies, such as those incubated by Crystal Ventures or Horizon Group, another Rwandan investment fund, one day sell shares to investors through IPOs. "In order to grow, we need products [i.e., stock listings]," Mathu said. With no additional privatization plans by the government at the moment, the exchange is turning to the private sector to stir up interest in listing shares. "We work closely with the [Rwanda Development Board]. Every time we see companies with potential, we try to bring them onboard. Whether they come today, tomorrow, or next year, we identify them," he added. "Since this is a new area, we need to give them time for education. By the time they start coming onboard to raise capital from the market, they will be ready."

The second area of growth for the exchange is cross-listing of companies whose shares trade primarily in another market, such as the much larger Nairobi Stock Exchange. "If investors want to buy an oil company operating in Kampala or Nairobi, they will find it trading here," Mathu predicted. Although the Rwanda Stock Exchange has a modest beginning, it is laying the foundation for a much bigger platform, including electronic trading of shares, which will be limited at first to computer terminals at the exchange. Backed by security laws that promote good governance, the exchange may also garner volume from institutional investors, particularly in cross-listed shares. Eventually, integration of capital markets across the East African region will promote cross-border transactions and could lead to greater trade volume, or liquidity, for the Rwandan exchange.

Renaissance Group, which specializes in emerging markets, underwrote the Bralirwa and Bank of Kigali IPOs. Although on a global scale these were relatively small deals, Renaissance Group CEO for Africa Clifford Sacks applauded the Rwanda Stock Exchange for being forward-thinking and promoting high integrity and professionalism among brokers, which could encourage trading on the Rwandan exchange rather than elsewhere in the region, where the anonymity of the buyer or seller is not always preserved. He extended his praise to Rwanda's business climate in general. Although still dwarfed by Nigeria, which is called the "China of Africa," Rwanda attracts interest because of its sincere desire to do things the right way. "The Rwandan government is trying to create the right backdrop for international investment," Sacks said.

Kagame clearly leads the way with a deep understanding and appreciation of the global business community. "When you look at his friends worldwide, he has more friends in the business community than in political circles," one member of his administration told us. "That relationship with the private sector makes it easy for us to unlock stumbling blocks for the private sector, and makes the private sector want to associate with him and this government."

At a Renaissance Capital–sponsored investment conference in Kigali in late 2011, institutional investors from around the world came to Rwanda, several for the first time. Although many initially associated Rwanda with the genocide, their last-ing impressions were more varied and future-oriented, observed Patrick Mweheire, CEO of East Africa for Renaissance Capital: "They walked away with an amazing feeling—energy and hope. People should come here and see for themselves."

There is another selling point for investment opportunities in Rwanda, beyond this market of 10.7 million people. Rwanda is part of the East African Community (EAC), with a combined population of 130 million people. The EAC comprises Kenya, Uganda, Tanzania, Rwanda, and Burundi, and has worked to foster political and economic unity by forming a customs union to allow for free trade in 2005 and a common market in 2010. The next phase would be a monetary union with a single cur-rency, and then potentially the formation of a political federa-tion of East African States.

Dr. Richard Sezibera, secretary general of the EAC, is Rwan-dan. He sees potential for integration in infrastructure, includ-ing energy, transportation, and air space, and also promotion of good governance standards across the federation. In public statements, Kagame has urged faster progress on EAC integra-tion, particularly with regard to elimination of nontariff barri-ers and establishment of a framework to promote public-private partnerships in the region to support large-scale infrastructure projects, like the East African railway.

When we asked Kagame about the EAC, he took a much more philosophical approach, noting that the integration which is being discussed by member states is already happening "even in spite of governments" by the people of East Africa. "The people of Uganda, Rwanda, Tanzania, and Kenya are already connected much more than actually governments allow them," he observed.

Although there are some concerns within the Rwandan business community about how a small country will compete with its much bigger neighbors, EAC integration appears to be a net positive for the country, particularly as it pursues foreign direct investment. The promise of access to a much bigger market through the EAC will be a powerful enticement for a foreign company to set up operations in Rwanda. "The integration of Rwanda in East Africa is a fantastic thing. It allows us to access a huge market," said Foreign Minister Louise Mushikiwabo. "That makes us an investment destination."

10

"ARIKO"

Rwanda on the World Stage

For such a small country, Rwanda casts an immense shadow. Having gone through one of the worst human-induced tragedies of the modern era without intervention from the West, Rwanda now stands in the harsh glare of the spotlight as it develops economically, socially, and politically. Undeniably, Rwanda has achieved an amazing turnaround since the 1994 genocide: economically, with strong GDP growth; socially, with policies and institutions that support justice and reconciliation; and politically, as it decentralizes its government and pushes responsibility and accountability to the local levels. It is a process—a transition—that may take a generation or more to fully achieve. Mindsets engrained in paternalistic thinking toward the government (and by extension to the aid organizations that governments of developing nations typically rely on for nearly everything) must be shifted toward self-reliance and self-determination. Human rights and free speech must be ensured for the long term. Rwanda must continue its efforts to improve relations with the media and to promote professionalism among Rwandan journalists, raising standards for ethics and independent reporting while also improving access to government information.

Experts we talked to describe Rwanda as a "democracy in the making" or a "fledgling democracy." "The success of how strong that democracy will be and how strong those democratic institutions will be," observed U.S. Assistant Secretary of State for the Bureau of African Affairs Johnnie Carson, "will be determined over the next half decade as the country deals with economic, political, and social problems."

As Rwanda matures, the strength of its institutions will factor significantly. According to a theory advanced by MIT economist Daron Acemoglu and Harvard political scientist James A. Robinson in their book *Why Nations Fail,* when nations develop inclusive political and economic institutions, they thrive. Countries that ultimately fail are those that develop "extractive" institutions, meaning they take away from the many and benefit only a few who are given the power and opportunity.[1] Rwanda, by our lights, is well on the road to developing inclusive institutions, particularly those that encourage critical factors like property rights and a market economy. Although it has a ways to go in terms of democratic institutions, including establishing a track record of multiparty elections, Rwanda appears to be on track for sustainable success.

Despite the progress, however, some Western voices still say, "but"—or, as the word translates in Kinyarwanda, *ariko.* No matter what Rwanda has achieved—being on track to reach many of its Millennium Development Goals, ranking third among African nations (behind South Africa and Mauritius) in the World Economic Forum's competitiveness report, elevating a million people from poverty in the past five years, and so forth—the word that follows such statements is often *but,* followed by criticisms of the government, particularly regarding free speech, political processes, and its strict genocide ideology law that makes it a crime to deny the genocide or stir up divisive rivalries.

When we asked President Paul Kagame about how Rwanda is viewed by the rest of the world, he showed a rare hint of irritation. He has limited patience for outside observers whose prevailing opinion, he believes, is "they know best, not us"; those who view themselves as "the only saviors." When Rwanda meets its needs through its own initiatives and partnerships with nongovernmental organizations (NGOs) that improve health and education and reduce poverty, then the view changes, he continued. "Then there is a 'but' because you have to bring it down a little bit. We can't be seen as the ones behind the good story. [The view is] nothing good can come from us. . . . So, you can get good results and still get a bad name."

Arguably, if Rwanda had languished in its former state of despair, teetering on the brink of collapse with only a lifeline of foreign aid, it would have a less complicated presence. The scrutiny Rwanda faces, some say, is due in large part to its success, which makes it a target in the eyes of its most vehement critics, including in human rights circles. For Rwanda, perceptions that it is a "miracle" turnaround country, instead of a work of deliberate and ongoing progress, put it on an untenable pedestal.

As Rwanda pursues its ambitious goals—and achieves them—the harshness of the spotlight will only intensify. Kagame's advice to those who work closely with him for dealing with such scrutiny is to "try to pick something positive out of it. I tell them, 'The positive thing in my opinion is that this pressure puts us on our toes. It [motivates] us to try harder . . . We are always trying to prove ourselves, so let's find some silver lining.'"

The president's attitude illustrates his drive to face adversity and avoid victimhood. Rwanda was victimized by the tragedy of genocide, from the colonizers who divided people, to the European powers that backed the regime, to the West that did nothing to intervene. But rejecting that victimhood, Kagame believes, is the only way for Rwanda to stand on its own feet. "I have noticed the world over that the leaders who are good leaders don't want to talk about such things as the wicked nature of colonization. They are forward-looking," observed former U.K. Prime Minister Tony Blair.

Rwanda also understands the "noise" of dissention and criticism that surrounds it, which falls into three groups. The first is comprised of remnants of the *interahamwe* militants and other extremists who committed the genocide, many of whom have taken refuge in the Democratic Republic of the Congo, Rwanda's violent and politically unstable neighbor. Some remnants of the architects of the genocide today also live abroad and have not yet been brought to justice. For example, in March 2011, after 17 years on the run, one of the alleged masterminds of the genocide, Bernard Munyagishari, was arrested in eastern Congo and charged with several counts, including genocide and murder as a crime against humanity. After his arrest, the International Criminal Tribunal for Rwanda said nine of those believed to be most responsible for the genocide were still at large.

"Everything starts with Rwanda's history in 1994," Foreign Minister Louise Mushikiwabo explained. "Rwanda's detractors right after the genocide were those who, one way or the other, were associated with the genocide—either directly responsible or their families and friends were responsible. For them, the [end of the] genocide is defeat, and that ideology dies hard."

The second group is comprised of disaffected and disassociated Rwandans, including some who were formerly close to Kagame and the RPF leadership but who fell out of favor and/or were accused of corruption or other crimes—some of whom today have made careers speaking out against the Rwandan government. Both of these groups have political motivation for wanting to discredit Rwandan leaders and tarnish the country's reputation. "We hear the noise," observed Bishop John Rucyahana, an Anglican spiritual leader in Rwanda and chairman of the country's National Unity and Reconciliation Commission. "You need to know that the noise is not just noise. It's very strategic noise."

The third group is outside observers, who save their sharpest criticisms for Rwanda's record on human rights. This is the group that uses the but—ariko—most effectively and often.

Human Rights Watch, a leading independent human rights organization, acknowledges the progress made in Rwanda, particularly with regard to economic development. "Rwanda has obviously made huge strides in rebuilding the country since the genocide, which entirely devastated the country in 1994. In a period of 18 years, which is a relatively short time, there have been quite extraordinary achievements with regard to development and economic growth," commented Carina Tertsakian, a senior researcher in the Africa division of Human Rights Watch, who specializes in Rwanda and Burundi.

At the same time, Tertsakian told us, progress in civil and political rights—including freedom of expression and freedom of association—have not kept pace with economic progress: "Our fear and the fear of other Rwanda observers is that, unless this issue is addressed, unless Rwandans can start expressing themselves without fear, then there is risk that progress in other areas could be undermined."

Needless to say, the Rwandan government takes umbrage with this view. "Some of these academics and researchers have made a living defining themselves as Africanists, who claim to know Rwanda and the region," Mushikiwabo continued. "They are very protective of their view . . . They think they know better than the Rwandans themselves."

The issue of free speech hinges largely on Rwanda's genocide ideology law, which the Rwandan government strongly defends even though it puts limitations on individual expression. In a July 2010 interview with *Newsweek,* Foreign Minister Mushikiwabo addressed criticism of the ideology law, saying, "You see in our 2003 Constitution the word 'unity' repeated so many times. What that means is you can be critical, you can bring up any subject for discussion, but please do not bring [up] anything that's going to divide us again. That's a decision that was made by the citizens of Rwanda, and that is not something that would make sense in other places. We cannot be rushed into allowing any kind of discourse, [especially] when it takes us back to where we were . . ." Mushikiwabo went on to refute the view that the genocide ideology law was being manipulated for political reasons to limit opponents. "We do as a government welcome dissenting voices and different views, but we have a responsibility to preserve that kind of stability, the kind of unity, we've been working on very hard for the last [18] years."[2]

Of course, this raises a question: at what point does honest disagreement on a policy or program become harmful dissent? Agreeing to disagree risks becoming a serious infraction under these circumstances. Like everything else in Rwanda, it's a work in progress.

Tertsakian of Human Rights Watch acknowledged the genocide as a fairly recent occurrence with events that traumatized the population. "It is my view that, not only in Rwanda but in any country that has gone through such extreme suffering, it takes several generations to get over that," she added. "So there is always going to be sensitivity and always going to be fear. That's natural."

One of the loudest outcries occurred after the August 2010 presidential election, in which Kagame was reelected with 93 percent of the vote. The three other candidates in the election were all serving in and considered closely aligned with the government. Criticism has centered on the government's use of its genocide ideology law against certain opposition candidates and to shut down publications charged with printing derogatory or divisive articles. This prompted the White House to express its concerns about the suspension of two newspapers, the barring of two opposition parties, and the arrest of several journalists.

In an interview with the *Guardian* in December 2010, Blair defended his support for Kagame in the aftermath of the negativity surrounding the presidential election, adding, "I don't ignore all those criticisms . . . But I do think you've got to recognize that Rwanda is an immensely special case because of the genocide."[3] In our conversation with Blair, he commented that the "politics around Rwanda are necessarily complex . . . Until the country reaches Vision 2020, there is inherent fragility there. Therefore, the worry is they could slip back. It's a bit of naiveté on the part of outsiders for not understanding just how difficult their situation is, especially with the Congo next door."

The Western press often portrays the Rwandan presidential election of 2010 as one in which all opposition was prevented from running. For example, an August 11, 2010, *New York Times* editorial charged, "President Kagame made it almost impossible for anyone else to seriously challenge him, much less win."[4] The candidate who has received the most attention from the press, however, was one who was barred because of allegations she used a political platform as a way to stir up old ethnic hatred in the country. Victoire Ingabire, chair of the United Democratic Forces (FDU-Inkingi), was charged in 2010 with financially supporting a terrorist rebel group in the Congo, causing state insecurity and divisionism, and denying the genocide. Four of her codefendants have pleaded guilty. During Ingabire's trial, which began in late 2011, Rwandan prosecutors charged she had only "pretended" to be a politician in the country's presidential race, the second such election held since the genocide. Ingabire, whom government prosecutors have allegedly linked to the Democratic Forces for the Liberation of Rwanda (known by the French acronym FDLR) in eastern Congo, accused her of "trying to bring war to Rwanda." The *New York Times*, reporting on the trial, said the government has accused Ingabire with using "e-mail, face-to-face meetings and Western Union money transfers to recruit Rwandan Hutu rebels in eastern Congo to form a rebel group that could infiltrate Rwanda. Prosecutors also said that Ingabire had sought to recruit thousands of rebels from within Rwanda itself."[5] Throughout the proceedings,

Ingabire has maintained her innocence and denied the charges, calling them politically motivated. A verdict was expected in September 2012.

The trial, which was well publicized both inside and outside Rwanda, highlighted a hot-button issue for the country: the presence of rebels in eastern Congo that threaten Rwanda's security. The Democratic Republic of the Congo, which is 94 times the size of Rwanda, has been a threat to the peace and stability of the region since the genocide. Rwanda appealed to the West in the 1990s for help putting down an insurgency caused by militants in the Congo; when no assistance materialized, it did the job alone. Rwanda launched several military interventions—some clandestine and others later sanctioned by the Congolese government—to neutralize the threat. This resulted in a series of allegations against Rwanda, including that atrocities and human rights violations were committed by the Rwandan troops.

In August 2010, a United Nations draft report was leaked to the French newspaper *Le Monde,* claiming that investigators from the UN High Commissioner for Refugees had uncovered human rights abuses in the Congo in the 1990s by Rwandan forces. The Rwandan government assailed the report, calling it "immoral and unacceptable," and "a dangerous and irresponsible document that under the guise of human rights can only achieve instability in the Great Lakes region [Rwanda, Burundi, Congo, Uganda, and Tanzania] and undermine ongoing efforts to stabilize the region."[6] According to the Rwandan government, the report was influenced by its outside detractors and enemies, who wanted to taint the country's image on the world stage.

The UN report also alleged Rwandan troops had raided Congo's vast mineral wealth of gold, diamonds, and coltan, a mineral used in making cell phones and computers. In January 2012, the Rwandan military announced the arrest of four senior Rwandan army officers—three generals and a colonel—on allegations of smuggling minerals from the Congo into Rwanda. A military spokesman said the officers were allegedly working with civilians who, in turn, were engaged in businesses in the Congo that violated Rwandan laws.[7]

The Congo issue reignited in mid-2012 when another leaked UN report accused Rwanda of allegedly backing a Congolese rebel group known as M23. The Rwandan government has repeatedly denied the allegations. Weeks later, Kagame and Congolese leader Joseph Kabila met during a meeting of the 11-nation International Conference of the Great Lakes Region, at which a neutral international initiative in the region was endorsed.[8] The international conference proposes a ceasefire and cessation of hostilities as part of political solutions to end the fighting in the Congo, in order to promote peace and stability in the region.

For Rwanda, the presence across the border of militants from the FDLR is an ongoing and extremely serious threat. Rwanda still lives in the shadow of the genocide, which is well within the personal memory of much of its population. Peace and stability have been hard won, but tensions remain. For that reason, Rwandan officials believe it is imperative to impose strict laws regarding genocide ideology. (Similarly, several European nations, including Germany, have Holocaust denial laws, which also prohibit the use of Nazi symbolism.) In Rwanda, any person or organization that denies the genocide or is seen as fomenting conflict or ethnic hatred faces arrest and strict punishment.

There have also been allegations linking the Rwandan government to death threats and killings of journalists and Rwandan oppositionists. Two particular cases involve a journalist who was killed in June 2010 in Kigali, followed a month later by the murder of the vice president of the oppositionist Democratic Green Party of Rwanda. Both incidents happened just a few months before the presidential election.

The reports are troubling, but in every case, the Rwandan government vehemently denies the allegations, calling them patently false. In our conversations, Mushikiwabo and other government officials described them as politically motivated, another attempt to taint Rwanda's reputation. Mushikiwabo said the murder of the Rwandan journalist in 2010 was committed by a man who has subsequently confessed to the crime, because of a dispute that went back to the genocide. "Now they say, 'Rwanda is killing journalists,' even though it's a transparent case: the guilty person confessed," the foreign minister added. "This is going to be in the human rights book for the next 50 years."

The Rwandan government and human rights observers dispute each other's account of what occurred, a debate that is beyond the scope of this book and its discussion of economic development. What is clear, many say, is the need for greater freedom of the press. Rwanda has made conscious strides to improve its relationship with the media, both inside and outside the country. "Media-government relations haven't been very good, but now I think that is changing," commented Minister Protais Musoni, whose previous responsibilities included media affairs. The international group Reporters without Borders, in its press freedom ratings, ranked Rwanda 156 out of 177 countries in 2011, up from 169 the year before. (In contrast, the United States was rated 47 and North Korea 176, while Finland and Norway garnered the top spots.)

Musoni listed a number of reasons for Rwanda's contentious relationship with the press inside the country. "One is professionalism; you had people in this sector who were not trained," he explained. "Second, there was little private sector investment in it. Third, which is also quite important, the government was not communicating effectively."

Another challenge is that the media can be used as a mouthpiece for factions with agendas of their own. Therefore, it's essential for the Rwandan media to set standards for factual and independent reporting. Internally, Rwanda is elevating professionalism within the journalism field through education and ongoing training, including the School of Journalism and Communication, which relocated from the National University of Rwanda in Butare to Kigali, where there are more resources available to journalists, including practicing professionals. A Media High Council has also been established to set standards and self-police the industry. As the current minister of Cabinet Affairs, Musoni also helps organize press briefings for ministers and encourages interactive dialogue, including reporters' questions sent via text message and email to ministers for follow-up. "As the government opens up more and communicates, information flows," he added. Symbolic of this move is Rwanda's decision to convert a state-owned broadcaster to a public broadcaster.

Further, to open dialogue and promote understanding, particularly among the foreign press, Kagame holds monthly open meetings with all journalists in which reporters sit in the cabinet chamber with him and other government officials and engage in on-the-record discussions. Some sessions go as long as three hours. During a session with a delegation from the International Reporters Project in November 2011, Kagame was asked specifically about media independence and press freedom in Rwanda. His response, according to a transcript provided to us, was that reforms are taking place to improve the quality of journalism in Rwanda and management of media issues. "Where we are coming from, every sector, including the media, is all work in development," Kagame said. "It's something that people have to be patient about and we keep trying to see how best we can move forward."[9]

Tertsakian of Human Rights Watch called reforms of laws governing the media "quite positive," adding that "at least on paper [reforms] would appear to be favorable to a more open environment for the media. But that has yet to be tested in practice." One of the lingering problems in her view, she added, is that "defamation remains a criminal offense."

There is other evidence of Rwanda's willingness to engage in dialogue with the outside world, including its critics. The president himself has become an active user of social media to speak directly to people without a journalistic intermediary. Kagame has about 70,000 Twitter followers and tweets regularly on subjects from leadership to soccer. (We were told by several people close to the president that Kagame composes and posts to Twitter himself, not through anyone else.) In May 2011, Kagame engaged in a very public Twitter debate with a foreign journalist, Ian Birrell, who had accused the president in a tweet of being "despotic & deluded." Kagame, according to one account of the exchange, shot back, "You give yourself the right to abuse [people] and judge them like you [are] the one to decide." A very heated exchange ensued, with Birrell charging that there is a lack of freedom in the press; Kagame, and later Foreign Minister Mushikiwabo, responded with Rwanda's accomplishments in terms of advancement of the Rwandan people and stressed that newspapers associated with "criminality" have no place in Rwanda.[10]

Reading through the transcript, which is posted online, what is so remarkable is that the debate occurred in such a public forum as Twitter—visible to the world and available in virtual perpetuity through the Internet. For a robust debate between a journalist critic and government leader to occur in real time— unedited and unmanaged—is extraordinary.

As the noise has continued to swirl around Rwanda, leaders have also faced persistent allegations, later proved false, that the Rwandan Patriotic Front was behind the assassination of former President Juvénal Habyarimana, and specifically that Kagame, as the RPF military leader at the time, had ordered Habyarimana's plane shot down in April 1994, just before the genocide erupted. Rwandan officials repeatedly denied the allegation as baseless and charged that Habyarimana was murdered by militant extremists. Yet these claims were picked up by the mainstream press as French officials continued an investigation into the incident.

Over the years, these allegations have created political standoffs for Rwanda, culminating with arrest warrants being issued in 2006 against members of the Kagame administration, including Rose Kabuye, a retired major in the RPF who served as chief protocol officer in the Kagame administration. In our discussion with Kabuye well after the fact, she spoke rather cavalierly about her arrest warrant as a minimal risk to her person. She refused to stop working or traveling, even though her children worried that she could be charged and imprisoned. Kabuye assured them there was no reason for concern, because she was innocent. A tip through political channels revealed a plan for Kabuye to be arrested when she passed through London on her way to the United States. There was no incident either en route to the United States or returning to Rwanda, and she continued to travel internationally on government business, going to South Africa, Dubai, and again to London.

Then, in November 2008, when Kabuye was in Frankfurt, Germany, on government business, she was arrested on the French warrant. Kagame visited Kabuye while she was held in Germany for ten days at a women's prison, and afterward told reporters her arrest "has some implications, foreseen or unforeseen, because in many ways it's a violation of the sovereignty of Rwanda."[11] Kabuye was then extradited to France, where she was kept under house arrest for several months before being allowed to return to Rwanda as the investigation continued. In protest of the arrest, Rwanda expelled both the German and French diplomats from Rwanda. Kabuye's arrest warrant was lifted in March 2009.

The allegations against Kagame and others in the RPF were silenced in early 2012, when an investigation team, mandated by a French court, determined that, based on the trajectory of the missile, RPF forces could not have been responsible for downing the former president's plane. The French team concluded the missile had been launched from the Kanombe military base, which in 1994 was tightly controlled by the former regime's elite presidential guard.

Officially, the Rwandan government welcomed the French judges' report as "vindication for Rwanda's long-held position on the circumstances surrounding events of April 1994." In a statement, Foreign Minister Mushikiwabo said, "It is now clear to all that the downing of the plane was a coup d'état carried out by extremist Hutu elements and their advisors who controlled Kanombe Barracks."[12] But speaking at a televised event in Kigali, Kagame subtly chastised those who breathed a sigh of relief over the French court's finding, reminding them that the country did not need any foreign authority to tell it what happened. His comments echoed remarks he had made in an interview with *La Liberation* in September 2011 while in Paris: "We did not sit back and wait passively for a foreign magistrate to judge us and tell us the truth. As for those who fired the missiles and their methods, the facts speak for themselves."[13]

Tellingly, rather than focus on the past, Kagame used the interview with *La Liberation* to press ahead with a new agenda regarding France, now that diplomatic relations between the two countries had been normalized. French President Nicolas Sarkozy visited Rwanda in 2010 and admitted that "grave errors of judgment" were made by his country during the genocide, although he stopped short of extending an apology. His comments were clearly taken as an olive branch; it was the first visit by a French head of state to Rwanda since the genocide. As reported by the press at the time, Sarkozy said France and the international community had "a form of blindness to not have seen the genocidal dimensions" of the former Rwandan regime. Now, he pledged, France would "construct a relationship of confidence."[14]

In the *La Liberation* interview, Kagame welcomed a partnership with its former nemesis. "France can invest in a range of sectors: energy, tourism, infrastructure . . . We need everyone to help us improve the lot of the population, which remains very poor." Asked if cooperation between the two countries could also be military, Kagame responded that "nothing should be ruled out; we shouldn't limit ourselves *a priori*. France has a role to play, especially in the social and economic field, and even in the military and security sector."[15]

As Rwanda moves beyond its tragic past, it embraces a larger role on the world stage based on its hard-won expertise in nation building and its track record of successes, which can serve as an example to others. Because of Rwanda's track record on poverty reduction, Kagame serves as cochair of the UN's Millennium Development Goals' (MDG) Advocacy Group. Rwanda was also among the African nations highlighted by U.S. Secretary of State Hillary Clinton for having "strong successes with their approaches to development." In a June 2011 speech before the African Union Commission in Addis Ababa, Clinton praised Zambia, Mali, Ghana, and Rwanda for achievements such as diversified economies, job creation across several sectors, and decreased poverty. "Based on lessons we've learned from our work around the world, the United States wants to deepen our partnerships with countries that take a broad-based, inclusive, sustainable approach to growth," Clinton added.[16]

Rwanda has also extended beyond its own needs to those of others, committing some 3,500 troops to UN peacekeeping forces in the Darfur region of Sudan, which has been ravaged by civil war and atrocities. "Rwanda has . . . continued to act as a responsible global citizen, contributing to regional and international peace and security: being the second largest peacekeeping force in the Darfur region in Sudan, and number six in the world in contribution to peacekeeping forces around the world," observed Donald Kaberuka, president of the African Development Bank and a former Rwandan government official.

In early 2011, as U.S., British, and French forces launched strikes against Muammar Qaddafi, who had evoked images of genocide to crush rebels seeking to overthrow him, Kagame was one of the first to speak up in favor of Western intervention. "No country knows better than my own the costs of the international community failing to intervene to prevent a state killing its own people. In the course of 100 days in 1994, a million Rwandans were killed by government-backed 'genocidaires' and the world did nothing to stop them," Kagame wrote in an editorial published in the *New Times,* a Rwandan newspaper. "Given the overriding mandate of Operation Odyssey Dawn to protect Libyan civilians from state-sponsored attacks, Rwanda can only stand in support of it. Our responsibility to protect is unquestionable—this is the right thing to do, and this view is backed with the authority of having witnessed and suffered the terrible consequences of international inaction." [17]

Kagame also observed that had the African Union supported Western intervention in Libya, such action "would have acted as a further deterrent to other African leaders who might be tempted to target their own people with violence." He added, "The uprising in Libya has already sent a message to leaders in Africa and beyond. It is that if we lose touch with our people, if we do not serve them as they deserve and address their needs, there will be consequences. Their grievances will accumulate—and no matter how much time passes, they can turn against you." [18]

Sitting in the presidential offices, Kagame reflected on what it means to him for the government to provide freedoms to the people. He feels such freedoms must be viewed as a whole in the context of the well-being of all the people, and not piecemeal. "Do our people have food on the table? Are our people able to express themselves and their choices? Are there results that impact their lives?" he asked. In Rwanda's case, the answer to those questions is a resounding yes.

According to a Gallup poll, Rwandans give high marks to several areas such as freedom of expression, belief, association, and personal autonomy (77 percent); a fair and honest electoral process (86 percent); preservation of the environment (91 percent); belief that hard work allows people to get ahead (93 percent); and confidence in the national government (95 percent, the fourth-highest ranking in the world).

Kagame seemed phlegmatic about the perceptions of his country—including those of most vocal critics—contending that, in the end, measurable and meaningful results are all the vindication he needs. "I would rather have tangible results and misperceptions than a good perception but nothing behind it," the president remarked. "If you have good perception, but nothing is real, it will be exposed."

This is the epitome of Rwanda's approach to the world stage in front of an audience that includes its critics and its fans. No matter what people say, pro or con, in the end the results are what matter. It's about the bottom line, focusing on the end game, and delivering for stakeholders, especially the Rwandan people. Kagame, ever thinking like a CEO, understands and embraces that fact. Tangible results, Kagame told us, are like one of his favorite sayings: "the truth goes through the fire." "The truth will never be destroyed," he added. "At some point, when the fire is out, the truth shows up. If the truth is real, it will overcome the misperception."

11

RWANDA LOOKS AHEAD TO SUCCESSION

I n spite of all that has been accomplished in Rwanda in less than two decades, for President Paul Kagame—as with so many high-profile leaders—one of the most significant things is how his term ends. In business and political circles, what can ultimately determine a leader's legacy is the smooth hand-off of power to a successor who has been properly groomed to take over. For Kagame, who has pledged to step down in 2017 after two democratically elected terms, how and when he leaves will be a defining leadership moment. On a continent that has suffered greatly from a lack of responsible leadership transitions, his succession in five years could be his ultimate legacy.

Based on our conversations with Kagame and other leaders in Rwanda, we expect the president to keep his promise. Although five years is a long time, and there is still much on Rwanda's agenda Kagame plans to accomplish, succession is vitally important, especially for the country to prove that it is developing democratic institutions larger and more important than any one individual. Ideally, by 2017 several candidates within the ruling party, the Rwandan Patriotic Front (RPF), will be developed enough through key leadership experiences to be viable successors. From that slate, one will be chosen to stand for general election, which, Rwandans hope, will include candidates from other parties as well.

A smooth, democratic transition in the presidency will put to rest the single biggest criticism of Paul Kagame: that he is a dictator. Critics have persistently chided Kagame for what they view as his stronghold on the country. That negative chorus will be silenced if he seamlessly passes the baton of leadership to the next president. Then he will be remembered most for what he did, which so many did not: complete an orderly, democratic succession.

Given Rwanda's remarkably swift progress, the stakes are high. Fitch Ratings, in its confirmation of a "B" credit rating for Rwanda, observed, "Mr. Kagame's lengthy rule and the stability it has brought highlight the importance of an orderly succession after 2017."[1] For Rwanda to fulfill the promise and potential of its Vision 2020, there must be strong leaders waiting in the wings who can finish what Kagame has started. Otherwise, Rwanda's gains could be jeopardized—even reversed—which could even undermine the stability of the entire East African region.

The same dynamic occurs in the corporate world. Much of a CEO's legacy rests on succession; ideally, the departing leader has identified multiple candidates who have been developed through the breadth and depth of varying experiences across an organization. A rough transition can tarnish a leader's record, no matter how impressive his or her prior accomplishments.

In a proper succession process, it is not up to the CEO to make the final decision; the board of directors continuously evaluates a slate of internal candidates and votes on a successor. (Hopefully, everyone can agree on an internal candidate, and there is no need for an external search.) However, a CEO who is retiring or otherwise leaving on his or her own accord can still have significant influence by recommending a successor.

Kagame will likely have a strong say in whoever is chosen by the RPF to stand for election, and he could ultimately be responsible for the selection and development of potential successors. When we asked Kagame about potential successors, he spoke confidently about candidates who could take over the leadership of Rwanda. "Even now, we have them, not that we have pinpointed a leader that I want or that is like me. Whoever comes after me will be different from me. Everybody is different," Kagame told us. "My job today and for the last so many years has been providing opportunities and exposing people to [new] opportunities."

Whoever the successor is, no one is exactly like Kagame, without whom Rwanda would not be as it is today. Kagame is a one-of-a-kind leader, which made the subject of succession difficult for us to broach with others. "I don't want to think about that," a Rwandan businessman said. "It's going to be very tough in terms of someone else meeting [Kagame's standards]. I don't see anybody to fill that place. I hope I'm wrong."

After a moment's reflection, the man's tone became more positive and assertive. "I am sure of one thing. Rwandans will be very confident about themselves. They have seen an example of strong leadership. After that, you can't take people backward." Kagame's leadership, he added, has become a high standard for others to follow, the benchmark by which future leaders will be judged.

"Kagame is the one who is thinking more about [succession] than anyone else," Rose Kabuye, who is now an independent businesswoman in Rwanda, told us. "He knows that it is better to go when you are strong and can help than when you are weak and cannot help. Everyone is saying, 'Who is [the successor] going to be?' As long as he is strong, the party is strong."

For Kagame, Kabuye added, the party is the top priority in the political process. Like political leaders everywhere who champion and believe in their parties, when Kagame speaks of the RPF, he describes it as embodying the goals and priorities of an entire country for unification, reconciliation, development, peace, and prosperity. "People have not become RPF by any other means than persuasion, by [showing] them the correctness of our political view and our political life," Kagame explained. "As they benefit through participation, we have turned them into stakeholders. The RPF has created an environment that has turned this country into a country with opportunities. We really broke this barrier, this divide of Hutu and Tutsi, and have created one tribe, which is being Rwandan and which is also being RPF. When you are in the RPF, you believe in the unity of the country."

Given the RPF's dominance in the country, it may be a given that the next president, whoever he or she is, will be from the RPF, although that is not to discount the presence of opposition candidates in the next presidential election. Indeed, as Rwanda's democratic electoral processes develop, it needs strong opposition candidates who will contribute to a healthy and productive debate about Rwanda's future, instead of inciting enmity of its tragic past.

Within the RPF, Kagame's influence over the choice of his successor will be invaluable to ensure that his successor shares his vision for the country, and is capable of executing on the country's next strategic initiatives—the makings of its "Vision 2030" and beyond. No frontrunners have emerged as yet, nor would it be timely to reveal them with five years left in Kagame's term. Whoever the likely candidates are, they are probably developing their skills and aptitudes outside the spotlight for now. There is also speculation, based on Kagame's own comments, that his successor should be younger than he (he will be 59 in 2017) and female. A woman, observers told us, would be more likely to be judged on her own merits than a man with a background similar to Kagame's.

As potential candidates are evaluated and vetted, the unintended consequences of Rwanda's strict zero tolerance for corruption may come into play. It is possible that capable candidates who have not breached any laws or ethical standards may decline to lead for fear that there could be even a hint of impropriety in their backgrounds, from close associates or family if not themselves. The downside of Rwanda's anticorruption stance is that a mere allegation becomes ugly and public very quickly, and even if proven false, it lingers as a stain on a person's reputation.

Although Kagame acknowledged it is his job to help groom a candidate, he stopped short of accepting responsibility for the outcome of that person's leadership. "I can only be responsible for what I have failed to do or what I managed to do," he added. "Maybe this is a bad proverb to use, but there is a saying when you are breeding puppies. You want to take care of them equally well, but you never know which one will turn out to be the best hunter. In breeding them, feeding them, and looking after them, if you don't do it equally well, you may miss out on the real talent. You keep doing it and enabling those who will be good to [emerge]."

If the next elected leader does not have the necessary capabilities or does not exhibit that he or she has the country's best interest in mind, the electoral process will take care of the problem, Kagame added. "The process is there, it is part of the culture," he explained. "If the person turns out bad, they will throw him out and bring in another." In the same way, a CEO who fails to execute a company's strategy or whose leadership comes into question because of poor results will inevitably face criticism from shareholders and pressure from board members to step down or be removed. In both politics and business, what matters most are the existence and health of processes that promote accountability.

Amid all the discussion about succession, there has been much speculation as to whether Kagame will seek a third term, even though to do so would mean changing the constitution. Some Rwandans may want to keep the status quo, while critics believe he will give into the temptation of clinging to power, as so many other African leaders have, including those who started out with the best of intentions. The publication *Rwanda Focus*, in an analysis published in August 2011, a year into Kagame's second democratically elected term, noted, "International commentators, journalists in the media, and ordinary people talking in private have been expressing doubts about Kagame's sincerity when he says he will step down come 2017."[2]

There are plenty of precedents, including Ugandan President Yoweri Museveni, who became president after a military coup in January 1986 and remains president today. *Rwanda Focus,* in its editorial, was adamant in its belief that a third term for Kagame was out of the question. "What all doubters seem to overlook are two traits that define Kagame more than any other: he is a man of immense self-discipline, and he is a man of his word. He will do what he said he will."[3]

Speculation around a possible third term heated up in particular during Kagame's visit to Uganda in late 2011, when he gave what appeared to be a noncommittal answer in response to a reporter's question. Kagame was asked to comment on talk about amending the constitution, which could allow him to run for a third term. "I will not be uncomfortable at all with people saying this or the other," Kagame said, according to news reports. That response, minus a denial that he would run for a third term, appeared to indicate that Kagame not only had no problem with amending the constitution, but actually welcomed it.

A closer look at his other comments, however, do favor another interpretation: that he was actually supporting people's rights to discuss political issues openly. "There's contradiction, on one hand you say people should have freedom to express themselves. On the other hand, you start questioning somebody expressing himself . . . It's as if people expect me to go to this person and say, 'You shut up. Don't talk about this anymore.' No. This is not my business," Kagame told Reuters.[4]

As speculation about a third term swirled into the headlines in early 2012, RPF leaders stepped in to clarify: the party was against amending the constitution to eliminate term limits or to introduce a third term to allow Kagame to stand for reelection.

"When we have a constitution written by people, debated by people, voted by people, and passed by people, in order to change it you have to have a very serious reason," Senator Tito Rutare-mara, head of the RPF, told the newspaper the *Chronicles*. The only example he gave was if the country were to be at war and there was no time to organize elections.[5]

At a national prayer breakfast in Kigali in January 2012, Kagame left little doubt he would step down in 2017, not with an emphatic denial of a third term, but with an admonishment: if other people think it will be time for him to go, Kagame re-marked rhetorically, then why would anyone assume he thinks differently?

A few days later, we met with the president, and told him we took him at his word that this would be his last term. "If you want, you can reserve that thinking until that day," Kagame said with a slight smile. Clearly he understood that no matter what he says now, people will not be convinced until after the election.

Meeting with a delegation of international journalists in No-vember 2011, Kagame used questions about succession to ad-dress broader issues about leadership and the role of the leader, not as one who is privileged but as one who shoulders a respon-sibility. Kagame stressed that, as discussed in Chapter 5, he never sought to become president. Rather, he served in that capacity because it was determined to be in the best interest of his coun-try. "I did not become president because it was something I was dying to be. Before I became president, I was somebody and I was satisfied to be what I was," Kagame said. "I am not a presi-dent because of privilege or anything else. Circumstances put me here . . . I can't sit here and say I must be president for life. . . .

Since I have lived without being president before, I can happily leave."[6]

He acknowledged that stepping down would also be in the best interest of the country and the principles of governance that have been established, with institutions that will outlive any one individual. "I mean what I say," Kagame continued. "When I struggled for my country and for my own rights and for my people's rights for many years, I did not do it as a matter of passing time. It was a serious investment, which has a meaning to me and to the people of this country. I, therefore, cannot be associated with anything that could result [in] reversal of these investments. I understand critics and I know what is right and wrong . . . I am not perfect; nobody is, but I think I can make a decent judgment and I know what is good for my country and my people. . . . Being in power is not something that I want so badly that I would do anything to be there."

These are the words of a servant leader who has put the needs of others ahead of his own. Thus, the question is personal, an allegation that he would put his own ambition and power above duty, responsibility, and the greater good of the country. "That's why I almost take it personal when people keep asking me whether I will change the constitution," he added. "But I will say I will be around as a senior citizen in my country to make my contribution, but not as president after 2017. I tell people to be patient until 2017 instead of misjudging for nothing . . . People should have faith, the same faith we had all along."[7]

The question of a third term takes on even greater importance because Rwanda lacks a history of democratic successions. Kagame's predecessor was the first president appointed by the transitional government, Pasteur Bizimungu, who led postgenocide from July 1994 until he was removed from power in 2000 when he faced corruption charges. His predecessor was Juvénal Habyarimana, whose leadership came to an end when he was killed in what many believe to have been a coup by extremist factions which then started the genocide. Before Habyarimana, Grégoire Kayibanda was the country's first post-colonial president, from 1962 until 1973, when he was deposed in a military coup by Habyarimana.

As the first democratically elected president of Rwanda, Kagame draws comparisons to George Washington, who, as the first president of the United States, was urged to accept a third term but declined. For Kagame, no matter how much pressure he faces to stay on, leaving after two terms would be a significant move toward building democracy and setting a powerful example for other developing countries, where far too many leaders cling to power to the detriment of the country. An example is Hosni Mubarak, who, after coming to power in Egypt in 1981, was hailed as a strong ally of the United States and willing to work toward peace with Israel. As Mubarak's regime continued, however, corruption and oppression prevailed. Today, what Mubarak is probably best remembered for are the 18 days of "Arab Spring" protests in 2011 that brought his three decades of rule to an end.

It is an unfortunate fact of life that power has a tremendous pull on people, and they all too often become defined by their positions. In the corporate world, it can be extremely difficult for a leader to contemplate life after the executive suite; losing that role, even if only to retirement, can be an insurmountable setback. The life of a CEO is enormously challenging and stressful, but the trappings can be significant: corporate jets, rubbing shoulders with the global elite, and breathtaking executive compensation. The change in status and identity after leaving the post can be deeply unsettling.

For a president of a sovereign nation, it is no doubt even more difficult to separate role and identity. And another common misconception that befalls leaders of turnaround organizations, whether corporate or political, is there is no one who understands the problems and challenges as clearly as they do. Thus the incumbent can convince himself that staying on is the only choice. For Kagame, who has led the ultimate turnaround, it could be tempting to succumb to this perspective, especially if there is some truth to the view that stability in Rwanda—which some have described as a powder keg of tensions—is best ensured under him.

Kagame may find another way to help the country in an advisory capacity or through involvement in the private sector after he steps down. We expect he will find a way to support his country from behind the scenes, as a public figure in private life. "Kagame is truly not about himself, and this speaks to his values. Other people are willing to be guided by him, but it's never about him," observed Michael Fairbanks, who is a close adviser of Kagame, as well as a Fellow in the Weatherhead Center for International Affairs at Harvard University and cofounder of the SEVEN Fund.

The five years remaining in Kagame's term become incredibly short when one contemplates what must be accomplished. He must create a middle class, while at the same time continuing to raise the lowest level to avoid a gap between an emerging group of "haves" and the ever-present "have-nots." Institutions must be strengthened and solidified. And development should not be limited to within Rwanda's borders; as we were told, it cannot be the best house in a troubled neighborhood. Within the East African Community, Rwanda's example of a private sector–led development with strong governance based on accountability and transparency can help elevate the region.

No one is more aware of these facts than Kagame, who knows he will not accomplish everything on his agenda before 2017. "I have high ambitions to accomplish to turn this country into a middle-income country or beyond that before I leave, but I know realistically things will not work out that way. But what I am sure of, and I'm happy with, is there is movement toward that and it will continue to take place," he told us. "My ambition would be [to move at] double or three times the pace, but my wish and what happens in real life may be different."

Paul Kagame has made his country into the Rwanda the world sees today: stronger, unified, and one of the best business climates in Africa, which is the next frontier for investment and development. After him must come another who will shape Rwanda's future. It will be up to this new leader to carry Rwanda forward through its next challenges, both seen and unseen. Thus, Paul Kagame's ultimate legacy will be realized long after he leaves the presidency, that Rwanda marches on.

NOTES

CHAPTER 1: RWANDA NOW

1. John Rwangombwa, "Rwanda Can Be Proud of Its Economic Progress," *Wall Street Journal,* February 10, 2012.
2. The White House, "Statement on the National Elections in Rwanda," August 13, 2010. http://www.whitehouse.gov/the-press-office/2010/08/13/st atement-national-elections-rwanda
3. Susan E. Rice, "Remarks at Kigali Institute of Science and Technology as Prepared for Delivery," November 23, 2011, http://rwanda.usembassy .gov/sp_11232011.html.
4. *Doing Business in the East African Community 2012,* World Bank and the International Finance Corporation, accessed May 25, 2012.
5. Valery Noury, "Rwanda Most 'Business Friendly' in East Africa," *African Business,* January 2012, p. 48-49.
6. Republic of Rwanda, *Rwanda Vision 2020,* July 2000, http://www.gesci .org/assets/files/Rwanda_Vision_2020.pdf.

CHAPTER 2: A NATION DIVIDED BY HATRED AND HORROR

1. Gérard Prunier, *The Rwanda Crisis: History of a Genocide* (New York: Columbia University Press, 1995), xii-16.
2. Stephen Kinzer, *A Thousand Hills: Rwanda's Rebirth and the Man Who Dreamed It* (Hoboken, NJ: John Wiley & Sons, 2008), 29.
3. Ibid., 31.

CHAPTER 3: MARCHING INTO HELL

1. Reuters, "Rwanda Battles Rebels to Control District Capital," *New York Times,* January 24, 1991, accessed April 26, 2012, http://www.nytimes .com/1991/01/24/world/rwanda-battles-rebels-to-control-district-capital .html.
2. Stephen Kinzer, *A Thousand Hills: Rwanda's Rebirth and the Man Who Dreamed It* (Hoboken, NJ: John Wiley & Sons, 2008), 94.
3. "Hutu Ten Commandments," Wikipedia, accessed April 26, 2012, http:// en.wikipedia.org/wiki/Hutu_Ten_Commandments.

4. Jane Perlez, "Violence Roils Rwanda's Embryo Democracy," *New York Times,* July 1, 1992, accessed April 26, 2012, http://www.nytimes.com /1992/06/01/world/violence-roils-rwanda-s-embryo-democracy.html.

5. Kinzer, *A Thousand Hills,* 104.

6. "From Rwanda Study: 'Serious Mistakes Were Made,'" *New York Times,* December 17, 1999, accessed April 26, 2012, http://www.nytimes .com/1999/12/17/world/from-rwanda-study-serious-mistakes-were-made .html

7. Ibid.

8. Roméo Dallaire, *Shake Hands with the Devil: The Failure of Humanity in Rwanda* (Philadelphia, PA: Da Capo Press, 2003), 255.

9. Donatella Lorch, "Rwanda Rebels: Army of Exiles Fights for a Home," *New York Times,* June 9, 1994, accessed April 26, 2012, http://www .nytimes.com/1994/06/09/world/rwanda-rebels-army-of-exiles-fights-for- a-home.html?src=pm.

10. Philip Gourevitch, *We Wish to Inform You That Tomorrow We Will Be Killed with Our Families: Stories from Rwanda* (New York: Picador, 1998), 19-21.

11. Lorch, "Rwanda Rebels."

12. Republic of Rwanda, *State Building in Rwanda,* background paper for "Peace & Stand Building: The Rwandan Experience," November 2011.

CHAPTER 4: RECONCILIATION AND UNIFICATION

1. Immaculée Ilibagiza with Steve Erwin, *Led by Faith: Rising from the Ashes of the Rwandan Genocide* (Carlsbad, CA: Hay House, 2008), 60.

2. Erik Møse, "Address by President of the International Criminal Tribu- nal for Rwanda, to the United Nations General Assembly," October 9, 2003, accessed April 26, 2012, http://www.unictr.org/tabid/155/Default .aspx?ID=1080.

3. PBS.org, *Rwanda Reconciliation,* April 17, 2009, accessed April 26, 2012, http://www.pbs.org/wnet/religionandethics/episodes/april-17-2009 /rwandan-reconciliation/2708/.

4. Republic of Rwanda, *State Building in Rwanda,* background paper for "Peace & State Building: The Rwandan Experience," November 2011.

5. National Unity and Reconciliation Commission, *Rwanda Reconcilia- tion Barometers,* October 2010, accessed April 26, 2012, http://www .nurc.gov.rw/fileadmin/templates/Documents/RWANDA_RECONCILIA TION_BAROMETER.pdf.

CHAPTER 5: RWANDA'S CEO

1. Paul Kagame, "The Backbone of a New Rwanda," in *In the River They Swim: Essays from Around the World,* ed. Michael Fairbanks et al. (West Conshohocken, PA: Templeton Press, 2009), 13.

2. Jeff Chu, "Rwanda Rising: A New Model for Economic Development," *Fast Company,* March 18, 2009, accessed April 26, 2012, http://www .fastcompany.com/node/1208900/print.

3. Alex Perry, "Rwanda's Rebel Reformer: Paul Kagame," *Time,* August 9, 2010, accessed April 26, 2012, http://www.time.com/time/magazine /article/0,9171,2007287,00.html.

4. Ryan Tracy, "Some Rules Work Only in Rwanda," *Newsweek,* July 25, 2010, accessed April 26, 2012, http://www.thedailybeast.com/newsweek /2010/07/25/some-rules-work-only-in-rwanda.html.

5. Perry, "Rwanda's Rebel Reformer."

CHAPTER 6: THE RWANDA MODEL

1. Romesh Ratnesar, "Who Failed on Haiti's Recovery?" *Time,* January 10, 2011, accessed April 26, 2012, http://www.time.com/time/world/article /0,8599,2041450,00.html#ixzz1o3Ugvlkq.

2. Jeff Chu, "Rwanda Rising: A New Model for Economic Development," *Fast Company,* March 18, 2009, accessed April 26, 2012, http://www .fastcompany.com/node/1208900/print.

3. Paul Kagame, "Audience with Delegation of the International Reporters Project," interview transcript, November 17, 2011.

4. Rwanda: Joint Governance Assessment Report, adopted December 9, 2008.

5. World Now, "How Did Rwanda Cut Poverty So Much?" *Los Angeles Times,* February 16, 2012, accessed April 26, 2012, http://latimesblogs .latimes.com/world_now/2012/02/how-did-rwanda-cut-poverty-so-much .html.

6. Ann Lineve Wead Kimbrough, "An Outcome-Based Examination of the Post-Genocide Rwanda Leadership Model on the Country's Financial Performance," dissertation, Argosy University, 2012 (pending).

7. Africa Governance Initiative, "Speech: At Stanford University Tony Blair Calls for a New Approach to a New Africa," May 18, 2012. http://www .africagovernance.org/africa/news-entry/speech-a-new-approach-for-a -new-africa/.

8. Rwanda: Joint Governance Assessment.

9. Kagame, "Audience with Delegation."

10. World Now, "How Did Rwanda Cut Poverty So Much?"

CHAPTER 7: RAISING THE BOTTOM OF THE PYRAMID

1. Paul Kagame, "Umuganda Is About Self Sufficiency," speech, November 26, 2011, accessed April 26, 2012, http://www.paulkagame.com/2010 /index.php?option=com_content&view=article&id=521%3Aumuganda -is-about-self-sufficiency-kigali-26-november-2011&catid=36%3Anews &Itemid=71&lang=en.

2. TED.com, "Bill Clinton on Rebuilding Rwanda," award acceptance speech, March 2007, accessed April 26, 2012, http://www.ted.com/talks /bill_clinton_on_rebuilding_rwanda.html.

3. Saul Butera, "Rwanda Coffee Revenue Grew 84% to $5.9 Million in First Quarter," *Bloomberg,* April 18, 2012, accessed April 26, 2012, http:// www.bloomberg.com/news/2012-04-18/rwanda-coffee-revenue-grew -84-to-5-9-million-in-first-quarter.html.

4. John Bridgeland, Stu Wulsin, and Mary McNaught, "Rebuilding Rwanda: From Genocide to Prosperity through Education," Civic Enterprises LLC with Hudson Institute, 2009.
5. Ibid.
6. Derick W. Brinkerhoff, Catherine Fort, and Sara Stratton, "Good Governance and Health: Assessing Progress in Rwanda," April 2009.
7. World Health Organization, *World Malaria Report 2011,* accessed April 26, 2012, http://www.who.int/malaria/world_malaria_report_2011/978 9241564403_eng.pdf.
8. Donald G. McNeil Jr., "A Poor Nation, With a Health Plan," *New York Times,* June 15, 2010, accessed April 26, 2012, http://www.nytimes .com/2010/06/15/health/policy/15rwanda.html.

CHAPTER 8: DEVELOPING FROM WITHIN

1. PBS.org, "Volcanic Killers," *Savage Planet,* accessed April 26, 2012, http://www.pbs.org/wnet/savageplanet/01volcano/01/indexmid.html.
2. ContourGlobal.com, "ContourGlobal and Lending Group Accept Prestigious Award for KivuWatt Project Financing," news release, February 14, 2012, accessed April 26, 2012, http://www.contourglobal.com/.
3. CAPA Centre for Aviation, "Rwanda's new airport an attractive proposition as RwandAir takes off," September 21, 2011, http://www.centre foraviation.com/analysis/rwandas-new-airport-an-attractive-proposition -as-rwandair-takes-off-59155, (Accessed April 26, 2012).
4. "RCAA in plans to upgrade Kigali International Airport," *Rwanda Dispatch,* January 2012.

CHAPTER 9: OPENING THE DOOR TO FOREIGN DIRECT INVESTMENT

1. Patrick McGroarty, "Visa Enters Partnership to Expand in Rwanda," *Wall Street Journal,* December 5, 2011, accessed April 26, 2012, http:// online.wsj.com/article/SB100014240529702047704045770784625335 19278.html.
2. "S&P Assigns 'B/B' Ratings to Rwanda; Outlook Positive," Reuters, December 29, 2011, accessed April 26, 2012, http://af.reuters.com/article /rwandaNews/idAFWLA083920111229.
3. "Fitch Affirms, Rwanda at 'B'; Outlook Stable," Reuters, August 23, 2011, accessed April 26, 2012, http://af.reuters.com/article/commodities News/idAFWLA405620110823?pageNumber=2&virtualBrandChan nel=0.
4. Bosco Hitimana, "From a Truck Driver to a King of Kigali," *Forbes Africa,* December 2011–January 2012.
5. Kenneth Agutamba, "Rwanda: 10,000 New Jobs Created in 2011," *Rwanda Focus,* April 16, 2012, accessed April 26, 2012, http://allafrica .com/stories/printable/201204170026.html.
6. Starbucks.com, "A Rwandan Coffee Worthy of Attention," blog entry, May 6, 2011, accessed April 26, 2012, http://www.starbucks.com/blog /a-rwandan-coffee-worthy-of-attention/1009.

7. Tom Allen, "Reaching the Goal by Observing the Rules: The Sanctity of Contract," *Daedalus Experiment,* Fall 2011, accessed April 26, 2012, http://www.daedalusexperiment.com/issue-2/reaching-goal-observing -rules.php.
8. Isoko Institute, "From the PAC: Rod Reynolds on FDI," interview, 2012, accessed April 26, 2012, http://isoko-institute.org/uncategorized/from -the-pac-rod-reynolds-on-fdi/.
9. IOL.com, Business Report, *MTN Buys Extra Stake in Rwanda Unit,* October 6, 2011, accessed April 25, 2012, http://www.iol.co.za/business /companies/mtn-buys-extra-stake-in-rwanda-unit-1.1152113.

CHAPTER 10: "ARIKO"

1. Thomas L. Friedman, "Op-Ed: Why Nations Fail," *New York Times,* March 31, 2012, accessed April 26, 2012, http://www.nytimes.com/2012/04 /01/opinion/sunday/friedman-why-nations-fail.html?scp=1&sq=Why %20Nations%20Fail&st=cse.
2. Ryan Tracy, "Some Rules Work Only in Rwanda," *Newsweek,* July 25, 2010, accessed April 26, 2012, http://www.thedailybeast.com/newsweek /2010/07/25/some-rules-work-only-in-rwanda.html.
3. Chris McGreal, "Tony Blair Defends Support for Rwandan Leader Paul Kagame," *Guardian,* December 31, 2010, accessed April 26, 2012, http://www.guardian.co.uk/world/2010/dec/31/tony-blair-rwanda-paul -kagame.
4. "President Kagame's Win in Rwanda," editorial, *New York Times,* August 11, 2011, accessed April 26, 2012, http://www.nytimes.com/2010/08/12 /opinion/12thu2.html.
5. Josh Kron, "Rwanda Lays Out Charges Against Ex-Presidential Hopeful," *New York Times,* September 9, 2011, accessed April 26, 2012, http://www.nytimes.com/2011/09/10/world/africa/10rwanda.html.
6. Paul Richardson, "Rwanda Slams Leaked United Nations Report on Congo Genocide as 'Malicious,'" *Bloomberg,* August 27, 2010, accessed April 26, 2012, http://www.bloomberg.com/news/2010-08-27/rwandan -government-slams-united-nations-report-alleging-genocide-in-congo .html.
7. Graham Holliday, "Arrested Rwandan Generals Led Anti-smuggling Drive," Reuters, January 19, 2012, accessed April 26, 2012, http://www .reuters.com/article/2012/01/19/rwanda-army-idUSL6E8CJ3SH20120119/.
8. Associated Press, "Congo, Rwanda Agree to an International Force to Combat M23 Rebels; AU Willing to Send Troops," *Washington Post,* July 16, 2012, http://www.washingtonpost.com/world/africa/congo-rwanda -agree-to-back-an-international-force-to-combat-m23-rebels/2012 /07/16/gJQAOjoCoW_story.html.
9. Paul Kagame, "Audience with Delegation of the International Reporters Project," interview transcript, November 17, 2011.
10. A View from the Cave, "Ian Birrell vs. Paul Kagame on Twitter," May 14, 2011, accessed April 26, 2012, http://www.aviewfromthecave.com /2011/05/ian-birrell-vs-paul-kagame-on-twitter.html.

11. Associated Press, "Rwandan Says Arrest of Aide Was Violation Of Sovereignty," November 12, 2008, accessed April 26, 2012, http://query.nytimes.com/gst/fullpage.html?res=9804E5DD173CF931A25752C1A96E9C8B63.

12. "RWANDA: Habyarimana's Killing a Coup D'état—Report," *East Africa News Post,* January 11, 2012, accessed April 26, 2012, http://www.eastafricanewspost.com/index.php/national-news/677-rwanda-habyarimanas-killing-a-coup-detatreport.

13. Thomas Hofnung and Jean-Pierre Marc Perrin, "Our Relations Must Not Be Polluted by the Past," *La Liberation,* September 13, 2011, (English translation made available on Rwandan government website, www.gov.rw) accessed April 26, 2012, http://www.gov.rw/our-relations-must-not-be-polluted-by-the-past,498.

14. Anjan Sundaram, "On Visit to Rwanda, Sarkozy Admits 'Grave Errors' in 1994 Genocide," *New York Times,* February 25, 2010, accessed April 26, 2012, http://www.nytimes.com/2010/02/26/world/europe/26france.html?_r=1.

15. Hofnung and Perrin, "Our Relations Must Not Be Polluted."

16. U.S. Department of State, "Remarks at African Union by Secretary of State Hillary Rodham Clinton," June 11, 2011, accessed April 26, 2012, http://www.state.gov/secretary/rm/2011/06/166028.htm.

17. Paul Kagame, "Rwandans know why Gaddafi must be stopped," editorial, *New Times,* n.d., accessed April 26, 2012, http://www.newtimes.co.rw/news/views/article_print.php?&a=39509&icon=Print.

18. Ibid.

CHAPTER 11: RWANDA LOOKS AHEAD TO SUCCESSION

1. "Fitch Affirms, Rwanda at 'B'; Outlook Stable," Reuters, August 23, 2011, accessed April 26, 2012, http://af.reuters.com/article/commoditiesNews/idAFWLA405620110823?pageNumber=2&virtualBrandChannel=0.

2. "Analysis: One Year Into His Second Term, What Does Kagame Have Up His Sleeve?" *Rwanda Focus,* August 23, 2011, accessed April 26, 2012, http://focus.rw/wp/2011/08/analysisone-year-into-his-second-term-what-does-kagame-have-up-his-sleeve/.

3. Ibid.

4. Elias Biryabarema, "Rwanda's Kagame Says Fine with Third Term Talk," *Reuters,* December 12, 2011, accessed April 26, 2012, http://af.reuters.com/article/topNews/idAFJOE7BB05U20111212.

5. Jean C. Tabaro and Assouman Ntakirutimana, "RPF Not Interested in Third Term—Rutaremara," *Chronicles,* January 15, 2012.

6. Paul Kagame, "Audience with Delegation of the International Reporters Project," interview transcript, November 17, 2011.

7. Ibid.

INDEX